CALIFORNIA REVIVAL

Vintage Decor for Today's Homes

Carole Coates
and Annie Dietz

Photography by
Stephen Francis

Other Schiffer Books on Related Subjects:
Catalina Pottery
Monterey Furniture

Copyright © 2007 by Carole Coates & Annie Dietz
Photography © Stephen Francis
Cover concept: Robert Benson
Library of Congress Control Number: 2006934466

Designed by John P. Cheek
Cover design by Bruce Waters
Type set in Benguiat Bk BT/Zurich BT

ISBN: 978-0-7643-2635-6
Printed in China

Published by Schiffer Publishing Ltd.
4880 Lower Valley Road
Atglen, PA 19310
Phone: (610) 593-1777; Fax: (610) 593-2002
E-mail: Info@schifferbooks.com

For the largest selection of fine reference books on this and related subjects, please visit our web site at **www.schifferbooks.com**
We are always looking for people to write books on new and related subjects. If you have an idea for a book please contact us at the above address.

This book may be purchased from the publisher.
Include $3.95 for shipping.
Please try your bookstore first.
You may write for a free catalog.

In Europe, Schiffer books are distributed by
Bushwood Books
6 Marksbury Ave.
Kew Gardens
Surrey TW9 4JF England
Phone: 44 (0) 20 8392-8585;
Fax: 44 (0) 20 8392-9876
E-mail: info@bushwoodbooks.co.uk
Website: www.bushwoodbooks.co.uk
Free postage in the U.K., Europe; air mail at cost.

DEDICATION

This book is dedicated to all the unsung artists, men and women alike, who formed the backbone of California's Spanish Revival prior to World War II. The Chounaird Institute students and instructors, the animators at Disney's Hyperion Studios (who considered themselves artists first—and were), the Catalina painters, the Malibu designers, the pottery and tile workers, and untold numbers of muralists whose work has long been whitewashed over; in other words, all the "Juan Intenoches" of this world (see *Terminology*). We celebrate the people whose names we may never learn, but whose contributions have educated, elevated, and illuminated this ongoing study, and whose optimistic messages still resonate.

Acknowledgments

We offer our gratitude and thanks to the following individuals, companies, designers, dealers, decorators, artists, and museums for their assistance with this endeavor. By generously sharing important collections, opening their homes to our photographers, designing and decorating in the style, and providing historical information and assistance, they have all added to the rich continuum that is the California Revival movement. Your contributions of time, effort, friendship, and advice made the creation of the book more fun than frantic. We thank our families for enduring two years of take-out food and sporadic frenzy and look forward to resuming what passes as normal life among passionate "California" collectors.

Adamson House-Malibu Lagoon Museum
Robert Benson
Mark Berry
Frank and Charles Buschere
California Heritage Museum
Brett and Michele Canon
Alan and Laurie Carter
Catalina Island Museum
Charles Chamness and Joni LaGoy
Jack Chipman
Betsy Connors
Bob and Barbara Crow
Beatriz Curran
John and Katy Dempster
Park Dietz, MD
Mike Duff
Deborah Escobedo and Jose R. Padilla
Dolores "Dee" Fisher
Gloria Fisher
Stephen and Nancy Francis
Marty Frenkel
Susan Frost
Chris and Laura Geer
Mike Gonzales
Tony Guenther and Norma Wilson
Shelia Grether-Marion and Mark Marion
Rod and Gina Guerra
Maxine and the late Clifton Graves

Larry Harris
Wayne and Cate Heck
Marguerite and Edward Hiraga
Steven Hoefs
Norman Karlson
Diane Keaton
Jerry Kunz
Sue Ann Langdon and Jack Emrek
Paul Lenaburg and Phil Rubin
Lucinda Lester
Karen Lievense
Larry and Monica Lindsey
Kevin and Laura Marks
Bill Noonan
John Rallis and Mary Lynn Bergman-Rallis
Joanne Reeves
Roger Renick
David Renton
Jackson Rosenfeld
Geoff and Alison Rusack
Rusack Vineyards
Bart and Yvonne Scott
Don Shorts
Steven and Debra Soukup
Rick and Cristi Walden
Mike and Netta Yaeck
Ladenna Young
Jennifer Zachman

CONTENTS

CALIFORNIA REVIVAL

THE MOVEMENT

Introduction

In the 1970s, a handful of fanatic collectors and antique dealers stumbled upon a secret. There was a treasure trove awaiting them in attics and old cabins, sold at thrift stores and estate sales, tucked away at the Rose Bowl Flea Market in California, and scattered around the western United States. It prompted a new kind of California gold rush, this time involving period California furnishings and ceramic arts instead of nuggets. This rediscovery and renewed appreciation of vintage furnishings, arts, and crafts made in California during the Spanish Revival of the 1920s to 1940s, commonly called the Golden Era by a small but passionate group, must have seemed odd to the mainstream Arts and Crafts dealers at the time. Why were these California people collecting colored pots and old tiles, worn and vaguely Mexican-looking furniture, and Spanish style ironwork? But there were greater problems with this new endeavor than what your neighbors thought; the stuff was really hard to find, there did not seem to be enough of it to go around, no one knew what to look for or what to pay for it and, in some cases, who even made it. Those were the pioneer days, before the field had collector books, price guides, computer searches, or on-line auctions. It was great fun.

Three decades later it's a different story. A growing interest in the Spanish Revival and California historic decor has led to big changes. Both the pioneers—primarily California natives—and the newer devotees to this movement's latest incarnation launched research, writings, museum shows, and appeals for information. Some created reproductions, and others started their own intrepid collections with enthusiasm and energy sparking an important movement of national interest. Word spread from California to New York, and the style became popular with top decorators, with movie stars on *Architectural Digest* covers. It attracted serious collectors who began to use these important vintage furnishings and even some high quality contemporary versions in their daily lives. This distinctive and unique decor has iconic resonance and has been aptly named California Revival.

Today, California is a large and varied state with a population of over thirty-seven million people from many different cultures. Innovation and creativity have always been characteristic of California in its trendsetting role in art, movies, fashion, craft, design, architecture, computers, science, and education. The Spanish Revival movement (frequently confused with the Mission, Craftsman, or Arts and Crafts movements which preceded it) started nearly a hundred years ago and reflected the powerful influence of artisans, craftsmen, artists, and progressives working from northern to southern California, who were drawn to the Golden State. It has been said that if California hadn't invented itself, someone else would have done it. The boosters and developers in 1900s California started people dreaming about eating oranges from their own trees, feeling temperate breezes as palms sway, and the glory of a parade of roses in January. Myths and invention—some with a grain of truth, some pure Hollywood fantasy—aided by doctors' suggestions about the healthful aspects of the climate, brought millions of people westward. The restoration and rebuilding of California's abandoned 18th century Mission chain from San Diego to Sonoma sparked the imagination of the country during the early 1900s and planted the seeds of the Spanish Revival movement. Mainstays of the California decorative style that resulted were Monterey furniture, made in Los Angeles starting in 1929, brightly colored tile and pottery made by numerous companies, and relaxed and family friendly architecture that enhanced the indoor-outdoor lifestyle. The furnishings were especially popular with movie stars, then as now, as a perfect blend of romanticized history in imagery, locale, and decor. Popular movies and books at the time inspired paintings and painterly scenic tile images of caballeros and charros riding high,

Vintage California postcard highlights the sights of the "Golden State."

campesinos toiling or sleeping, and señoritas dancing at an apparently endless round of fiestas. The book *Ramona* by author Helen Hunt Jackson—an early activist for Native American rights—was a bestseller. The bright and primary colors of Catalina tile and Bauer pottery echoed the colors found in nature and the sun-saturated hues of the state's sea and sky. To someone pondering a move from the dustbowl states it must have seemed like a colorful mirage. The wonder is that the state's population explosion took anyone by surprise. Labeled accurately as the "Progressive Era" by California historian Kevin Starr, the infectious energy and can-do attitude of the times made it seem like anything was possible: building dams, freeways, houses; undertaking beautification projects: creating murals: writing screenplays and novels: studying mining and ceramics: and developing many other major industries prior to and throughout the Depression and the Works Progress Administration [WPA] era that followed. It seems cultural historian William Irvin Thompson's statement is true: "California became the first to discover that it was fantasy that led to reality, not the other way around."

Exploring California Revival decor, no matter where you live, inevitably involves learning some background about its Spanish Revival roots. Since it is an outgrowth of this classic style in architecture and design there is a brief history of the Spanish Revival later in this book, but the main focus here is on original and authentic California period furnishings, with a nod to San Antonio, Texas, the home of the various San Jose Workshops. Any mention of architectural style will be in relationship to decor or in expressing appreciation of the groundbreaking work of some of the classic architects such as Paul Williams and Reginald Johnson whose work is featured here. Following in the very large footsteps of George Washington Smith, Richard Requa, Julia Morgan, Gordon Kaufman, Wallace Neff, Cliff May and the aforementioned Williams and Johnson, many contemporary award-winning architects recognize these historic traditions in their work, evolving from modernism toward an evocation of what has become a true California style.

Whether your home is Spanish, Mediterranean, Mexican, Mission, Craftsman, Arts and Crafts, Ranch, Modern, Cabin, Lodge, or even European hotel style, California Revival decorative arts can be part of your interior design scheme. Contrary to common wisdom, you don't need a classic Spanish home to use California Revival style, nor does it belong only to the Western genre. It's a versatile look that can be achieved by taking advantage of the great "bones" of a historic home or by accessorizing in a contemporary rooftop garden, 1960s ranch house, high rise penthouse or condominium. It is hoped that this book will provide a point of reference for decorators, do it yourselfers, dealers, and collectors, a knowledge base for creating your own look, a bit of a contribution to the history, sociology, and urban archeology of the region, and an exploration of this enduring California style and art that was formed at a unique point in time in an amazingly rich setting.

The important contributions of Mexican craftsmen, artists, and designers and the great influence of Hispanic culture on the California style have been downplayed or ignored too often and for too long. California Revival enthusiastically embraces California's Mexican art and craft heritage along with Spanish, Native American, and rancho traditions. Sometimes serious, sometimes with a touch of irony, or with an explosion of fun and liveliness, California Revival decor reflects a hopeful and joyful approach to life.

This book seeks to share a vision of the current reality, richness, simplicity, and uniqueness that California Revival decor brings to the California architectural idiom and to show why it's making collectors, decorators, and curators from all over the country take notice. We agree with California architect William Wurster who said that for people, architecture is "the picture frame and not the picture." From elegant to rustic, from Manhattan to Oregon, from California to Florida, and New Jersey to Arizona, whether seen from a historic or a fantastical perspective, California Revival is a great way to frame an easygoing lifestyle.

Majestic Palm trees planted in 1904 line the main road at exclusive Hope Ranch along the Santa Barbara Coast and seem to welcome us.

CALIFORNIA REVIVAL:
THE LOOK

Vintage and Contemporary Homes
Spanish Revival, Mexicana, California Ranch, and Mediterranean

Your initiation into California Revival style begins with the outdoor elements that are the hallmarks of this look. Colorful designs in tile are an essential part of the entry, courtyard, patio, or pool in California Revival homes. Found in graceful fountains, pathways, stair-risers, planters, embedded in stucco walls, or as easy add-ons via iron frameworks, they are often accented by vivid garden pots, urns, and birdbaths. Inventive tile gaming, dining, and occasional tables invite outdoor living, playing and eating. Hand turned wooden gates, staircases, and shutters, and rough, hand hewn wooden ceiling beams and posts continue as thematic elements indoors as well. The use of metal is an easy way to add a decorative touch with hand wrought ironwork gracing handrails, lighting, benches, chairs, mural surrounds, and plant holders. An artisan's approach to stonework, custom concrete, and an emphasis on California-themed plants and landscaping makes for a well-rounded approach.

Next, a visual tour showcases ten real homes in both the city and the countryside that epitomize the California Revival style in all it's various permutations. Starting with a classic traditional look and continuing to the most dramatic, all shot in natural light—each has its own special flair. Going room by room from the entry to the living room, through the kitchens and dens, bedrooms, baths, and home offices with a few outdoor scenes for reference, this section will pinpoint accessorizing elements and themes, showing you how vintage decorative arts and furnishings made in California, as well as high quality reproduction and replications, can be used. We feature period and new custom homes in California from the Sonoma Wine Country to Newport Beach with detailed images in our Decorative Arts section. In addition we examine many rooms and museum worthy collections from five additional homes, including a Catalina condominium and a California Hacienda, and exteriors from scores more. We have chosen as examples everything from spacious homes built by famous architects to quaint country ranches and smaller, Spanish style cottages. We will show how individual collectors and decorators have infused the style with their own collecting interests through a harmonious blending to achieve looks that range from an elegant sparseness to a playful color bomb and everything in between. You will see an amazingly diverse selection of extremely rare and some easy to find pieces from homes where there is yet another unifying theme: these *are* homes and not just houses, where people, along with playful kids and muddy dogs, live.

Lastly, for the more studious, we will give a brief historical background on the Spanish Revival. Look for the *Terminology* section to help identify the California artists, manufacturers, potters, and related decor, and for a section on *Decorating Ideas*. You can also visit the book's web site to learn about the latest resources and reproductions, or go to our blog and contribute to ongoing research, discoveries, and resources.

Detail of fountain showing use of vintage California tiles.

Opposite page:
Outdoor fountains with vintage tile were once commonplace. Here it's an exceptional feature of this elegant home, doubly enjoyed when viewed from the living room or the nearby dining patio.

A courtyard version of a Malibu-style *Neptune* fountain created with reproduction tiles and an oil jar, found at a private home on Catalina Island.

A contemporary poolside fountain in reproduction tiles done in the Malibu-style in Newport Beach, California. The famous original *Peacock Fountain* can be seen on public tours given at the Historic Adamson House in Malibu, California.

A wall fountain in bright California colors with reproduction Moorish style tiles would work inside or out for an accent or where space is a premium.

Vintage Gladding McBean birdbath with a frog fountain accent is surrounded by Bauer flowerpots and tucked into a courtyard.

A grouping of vintage birdbaths: one by Pacific Pottery (tall blue), and two versions by Gladding McBean with various frogs, backed by salvaged Monterey style gates from Catalina Island, part of graphic artist Otis Shepard's original design theme for Catalina's old California look.

A swimming pool has colorful company in these large ringed jardinières made by Bauer Pottery in the 1930s. Reproduction tile used around pool edges and tile "dot" accents in surrounding terra cotta pavers.

Detail of seahorse topiary, formed concrete pots, and fencing.

Mature trees surround a lush pool. Unusual, formed concrete was used for the low border fencing, flowerpots, pedestals, walkways, and faux wood pergolas.

Detail of wall
fountain figure with
vintage Bauer pot.

Lush garden pond with figural wall fountain in background provides a quiet and shady retreat. An arched wall with columns capped in contrasting materials catches the eye.

Contemporary Spanish style home patio has all the hallmarks of California Revival style. Arched doorway, tiled
stair risers, California colors and plantings, indoor-outdoor
living spaces, and ornamental ironwork.

Detail of stair risers
done in reproduction
California tile.

Stucco planter bed is embedded with vintage California tiles and solid accent "dots" placed at attractive angles.

Made during the WPA era by one of the San Jose Workshops of Texas (1927-1977), this large tile mural depicts quaint village scenes in Mexico. Considered a "kissing cousin" of California style and design, many San Jose (*not* San Jose, California) tables and decorative arts made their way to California, then as now. Two vintage Catalina patio tables flank bench.

An iron bench topped with vintage Malibu tiles, a ship tile seatback, and three vintage Malibu floral murals on the patio wall.

Vintage Catalina backgammon table is nestled under a vine-covered trellis and surrounded by multicolored vintage Bauer hanging and standing flowerpots.

A bright stucco wall showcases an ornamental iron plant holder with vintage Bauer pots and succulents.

Curvy red roof tiles, soft white stucco, muted green trim, and "Bird of Paradise" plants bring a Santa Barbara look to the exterior of this home.

California Revival landscaping often uses decomposed granite driveways and paths. Plantings here tend to be mature olives, palms, agaves, and cypress in a Santa Barbara style. Topiary and raised concrete dividers evoke a formal simplicity.

Backyard barbequing with a twist: Catalina backgammon planters and a Hillside Pottery *olla* (oil jar) grouping.

A vintage Bauer terra cotta Indian pot stands atop a gated backyard entrance. The pots were secured to the post through the drainage hole.

Vintage Hillside Pottery, made of formed concrete with inset multicolored tiles, works well on this contemporary glass table and is another mainstay of the California Revival look. A concrete Madonna and child garden statue in background.

Pacific Palisades Classic—
The Ballin House

California Revival is showcased magnificently in this traditional Spanish style masterpiece. It has a classic California provenance and is outfitted with impeccable vintage California decor to match.

"The Ballin House" in Pacific Palisades is befitting of its original owner, designer and builder, Hugo Ballin. Ballin was best known as a painter, novelist, and director and producer of over 100 silent films. His most renowned work was his large scale, themed murals that grace some of the most famous buildings in Los Angeles, including the rotunda of the Griffith Park Observatory, the sanctuary of the Wilshire Boulevard Temple, the lobby of the Los Angeles Times building, the exterior tile mosaic of the Los Angeles Design Center, and the ceiling of the USC Medical Center.

Built in 1928, the Ballin House is done in the Spanish style so popular at that time, and features the tall and wide expanses that characterized this artist's work. It was one of the first homes built in the Huntington Palisades area of Pacific Palisades, on a wide street lined with mature eucalyptus trees. It is only a short hike away from the homestead and Polo Fields of Will Rogers, where Hollywood royalty

Vintage postcard Will Rogers Ranch House.

Designed and built in 1928 by muralist Hugo Ballin, this home exudes the uncommon grace that only good architecture and time can bestow.

and political bigwigs alike came to visit the famous wit, who'd never met a man he didn't like. Rogers fancied Monterey furniture, and his original California Revival decor (along with a few cowboy touches) still graces his restored home, now a Historic California State Park.

The original Ballin house features a living room and dining room with fourteen-foot high, beamed ceilings. Large combination French doors lead to a generous courtyard, allowing the residents to take advantage of the famous indoor-outdoor California lifestyle that the great weather allowed year 'round. A voluminous two-story studio features a tall north-facing window, and was probably the perfect spot for Ballin to work on his murals and paintings.

Perhaps drawn to the artistic pedigree of the Ballin House, the next owner was composer Vernon Duke ("April In Paris," "Autumn In New York," "Taking A Chance On Love") and his family. Duke used the studio space as a

musical staging area where he kept his two grand pianos, and invited luminaries such as George and Ira Gershwin and Bobby Short to visit and work.

Returning to the historically accurate California Revival furnishings that reflect the origins of the Ballin House, the current owners have collected California furniture, furnishings, and paintings from the 1920s, 1930s and 1940s that reflect, resonate with, and complement the architecture of the home. This includes Monterey, Coronado, and Imperial sofas, chairs, tables, and beds; Navajo rugs; colorful Catalina, Gladding McBean and Pacific pots; Batchelder, Claycraft and Malibu tiles; Bauer dinnerware; California plein air paintings, and yes, even a painting by Hugo Ballin. Although the proud homeowners don't claim to share the artistic credentials of Ballin and Duke, they do say that their young daughters show much promise as they sing, dance, draw, and paint throughout the house.

Three large Bauer terra-cotta Indian jars filled with colorful bromeliads sit on Mexican pavers. Doors that lead into the garden are detailed in bronze hardware and are original to the home. Earthy tones are used on the color-banded linen draperies.

Moroccan style ironwork entry gives view to large cobalt blue oil jar by Gladding McBean c1930s. Mexican pavers lead to oversized, wood paneled front door.

Formerly a music room, this great room now includes home office space in an added loft area. Fine examples of Monterey Furniture, manufactured by the Mason Manufacturing Company, Los Angeles, c1927-1945, vintage Spanish style iron chandelier, Native American rugs, open wood beam ceiling, and colorful tile stair risers are highlights of this spacious room.

Close view of Monterey sofa with gate leg side tables in old red painted finish. Heavy glass on top of a Monterey bench transforms it into a coffee table. Library area of the great room houses the owners' antiquarian books and was made from vintage lawyer's cabinets original to the home. Built-in alcove displays a small drum collection.

Below:
Detail of floral painting on back of classic Monterey couch. Rope work was used on some sofas and chairs and is a popular feature of the line today. Originally some female customers complained that the rope made their hosiery run, and so it was later replaced with metal strapping. The "Monterey" name is often found branded into the wood, as is their horseshoe logo.

Bottom right:
Detail of rope strapping visible through glass top on early Monterey bench, painted in straw ivory finish with primitive floral design.

These stair railings were custom-painted to replicate vintage Monterey furnishings. Tile risers are reproductions of vintage California tiles. Three vintage terra cotta oil jars sit on the Mexican paver floor.

Left: Detail of custom painting in Monterey-style colors.

Far left: Reproductions of 1930s style California tiles on stair risers. Preservation of historic period tile is an important reason to consider using reproduction tile for most permanent installations.

Detail of vintage triple-banded iron, Spanish-style chandelier. Small arched window shows off the deep-set walls and provides subtle lighting for high wood beamed ceiling.

Side view of Monterey buffet boasts fine example of hand painted floral designs that have distinguished Monterey furniture. Arched closet doors match vintage Monterey ironwork and paint.

An old California oil painting c1930s hangs above cinnamon-colored Monterey buffet. Hand thrown twist handle vases by Bauer artist Matt Carlton sit with three small Catalina Island vases and Indian basket. Glazes were named to evoke Island colors: Catalina blue, Toyon red, and Descanso green. Large ringed planter in original wood stand by Catalina Island Pottery. Iron floor lamp by Monterey. The scalloped ledge with wood beams was added during remodeling to echo authentic architectural details.

Iron leaf detail in orange paint on Monterey buffet.

Scarce Monterey prohibition cantina bar, sometimes called a tequila bar, with bottom portion and interior painted in crackle technique. The doors are in a medium brown finish for a striking two-tone effect and, when closed, give the appearance of a simple cabinet—a useful feature during Prohibition times. Scalloped green metal shelf has tulip design florals and Monterey iron hardware.

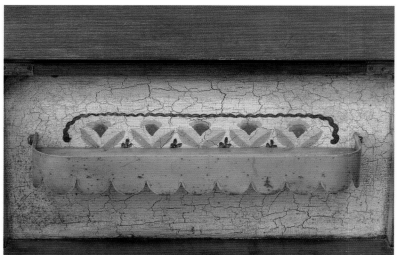

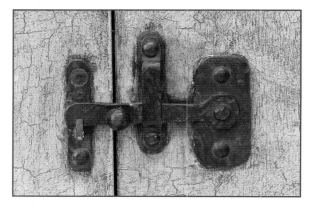

Above:
Detail of original tulip floral hand painting and metal shelf for glasses and liquor storage in the Monterey cantina bar.

Top right:
Detail of floral interior Monterey cantina bar shows Mexican-style floral painting and crackle-textured paint unique to Monterey furniture.

Right:
Hand hammered iron latch detail on Monterey cantina bar.

Detail of metal shade shows one of many unique designs used by Mason Manufacturing on Monterey furniture.

Monterey Buckaroo loveseat with Arts & Crafts period embroidered linen pillows. Spanish hacienda oil painting from the 1930s hangs on textured walls with wood wainscoting faux painted to mimic tiles. Monterey table lamp with wrought iron legs and metal shade.

Cozy corner of great room with comfortable Monterey armchair fitted with leather cushions in a warm brick red color to match painted metal shade on Monterey floor lamp. Oil painting of Mexican hacienda c1930.

New stainless steel and red enamel Viking gas stove provides a counterpoint to the vintage look of the reproduction Monterey cabinetry.

Roomy remodeled kitchen shows custom painting and replica ironwork in the Monterey style. Glass front doors allow for viewing of colorful vintage pottery. Scalloped shelf above sink houses a variety of vintage pottery ball pitchers. Countertops are tinted concrete and the contemporary tile back-splash has strategically placed vintage California Claycraft accent tiles.

Detail of Monterey-style painting and iron added to contemporary kitchen cabinets.

Close up of Claycraft tile accents from the 1920s alongside new tile in kitchen backsplash.

Detail of painted glass doors in kitchen cabinets with built in shelving. Bauer Matt Carlton twist handle vases in cupboard and Bauer ringware spice jars, salt & pepper and custard bowls set in wire rack sit on kitchen counter.

Detail of Mexican style crackle and floral motif hand painted on vintage Monterey A-frame kitchen chairs.

Monterey breakfast table and A-frame chairs accented with flower motif. Monterey triple light hanging fixture with hand painting on base and large metal shade. Bauer ringware bowl in Chinese yellow.

Monterey keyhole bed in straw ivory with painted florals, c1930. Vintage Native American Indian rugs, textured contemporary fabrics in Mexican serape colors for bedding and drapes. Monterey wine cellar chair in old wood finish.

Painted Coronado furniture desk and matching bench. Framed vintage Cal Art scenic Mission tile. Mexican tourist pottery vase has the Petitillo style popular in the 1930s.

King beds did not exist in the 1930s, so this one was created by joining two compatible Monterey singles. Wrought iron swing arm reading lamps hang over a pair of hand painted bed stands by Monterey. Details include an Old California plein air oil painting, an unusual Tramp Art box, and a rare Monterey trunk in old wood finish, which provides added storage at foot of bed.

La Cañada—
Paul Williams Playhouse

Nestled at the base of the San Gabriel Mountains this historic La Cañada compound features three wonderful 1929 Mediterranean structures designed by the renowned architect Paul Williams. Williams, considered by many to be "the last word in elegant traditionalism," was an outstanding and prolific African-American who worked in many styles in Los Angeles and throughout the world until his passing in the 1980s. He was known as the "designer to the stars" and his celebrity clients included Frank Sinatra. Originally built for famed L.A. Attorney James E. Degnan, of the firm Lawler and Degnan, the property was pictured in the Los Angeles Times in 1929. The article, headlined "Alta Canyada [sic] Activity Grows," showed a picture of the main house with the caption "Building activity is increasing this spring in Alta Canyada residential subdivision between Pasadena and Glendale. The accompanying home of sixteen rooms, to cost $125,000, is being constructed for James Degnan, attorney." It's possible that the impending economic depression as well as water shortages at the time curtailed the promising development, but many grand homes were built in the area since the moneyed class found it an easy commute to downtown Los Angeles following significant roadway and bridge improvements.

La Cañada is located in a natural bowl in the San Rafael hills outside of Los Angeles, near Pasadena and Flintridge. It's also home to a prime attraction, the secluded Descanso Gardens, which covers over 160 acres and includes a Japanese Tea House, a Live Oak Forest, a five acre rose garden, a Camellia garden, and the California Gardens, a nine acre section of trees, and plants native to southern California, all open to the public. It is a popular film location used most recently for "Memoirs of A Geisha" and "Legally Blonde." La Cañada is also home to the Jet Propulsion Laboratory, known as JPL. Managed by Caltech, it is NASA's lead center for robotic exploration of the solar system.

The magnificent La Cañada compound, comprising almost two acres, has a large, formal home as well as a pool house and another residence the owners refer to as the "Playhouse." Anecdotal evidence indicates the playhouse was built for the original owners to live in, perhaps as early as 1927, while the main house was being built. We will show you decorative elements, inside and out, from both, with the main focus on the wonderful turreted three-story playhouse with open-beamed ceilings in the great room, along with a fabulous faux-wood and river rock fireplace, and original touches.

The owners were very lucky to find the property as a kind of "white elephant" overrun with ivy and in all original, though somewhat neglected, condition. They

Vintage bridge scorecard with Spanish dancers.

have been dedicated to preserving and restoring the house to its original grandeur, a job that to our eye has been accomplished. Hidden under the ivy they found many unique garden folk art and furniture pieces that had been hand crafted for the home and have reinstalled them in their proper places. They also decided to furnish this smaller house with Monterey furniture and accents of Catalina pottery and period California art, since it was appropriate both to the vintage and to the old California style of the playhouse. Today it is a great place for kids or adults to watch the big screen television in comfy sofas tucked away in the back room, while also providing a nice open place to socialize and visit. Tile murals by Taylor Tilery feature Indians on the plains, Indian rugs are found here and there, and oil paintings introduce a Mexican motif that blends wonderfully with the colorful pottery and tile.

Back in the day, now obscure leading man Dennis Morgan, famous then for his singing "My Wild Irish Rose" in the movie of the same name, lived here during Hollywood's glamour era and hosted many parties with Hollywood luminaries, his pals and co-stars, such as Errol Flynn, James Cagney, and others, in attendance. The property originally encompassed six acres, with vineyards on the grounds. Mr. Morgan held grand affairs with his guests seated in the vineyards or enjoying the lake that reportedly used to exist on the property.

Set in a heavily treed section of suburban La Canada-Flintridge, the playhouse has enormous windows that frame the unobstructed view of the Angeles National Forest. The setting is serene and peaceful, and is a wonderful place to enjoy nature. The gardens boast nearly 100 types of old and modern roses, an abundance of fruit trees, and an organic vegetable garden that provides the family and their friends with fresh fruit and produce in the summers. The exterior features an Olympic-sized pool, topiaries, a cactus garden, dressing rooms, garden follies, numerous fountains, ponds, faux bois, and exotic mosaics of both glass and vintage California tile, with grottoes liberally sprinkled throughout the gardens. Look in the *Decorative Arts* chapter and the *Introduction* of this book for more amazing details in ironwork and exterior. We think you'll agree it's a unique, stunning property that never ceases to delight the mind and the senses.

Located on a historic compound built in the late 1920s, the turreted "Playhouse," a 4000 square foot home, is companion to a much larger main house. Both are featured here, as well as the unique hardscape, fountains, and gardens found on this special property.

Spacious great room with high, beamed ceiling and traditional large, paned windows give view to garden and mountains. Sofa, wingback chair with ottoman, bookcase, and coffee table are by Monterey Furniture c1930s. Brown and mustard Indian rug on sofa, c1940s, a pair of matching Spanish Revival chandeliers, and a contemporary kilim rug create an island for seating area.

Period faux-wood concrete artistry is found on this unique fireplace mantel with natural river rock surround. Tall 18" Catalina oil jar, bulbous vase, and two-handled vase in Toyon red, with a colorful Taylor Tilery oxen scene mural, c1930, atop mantel, with the owner's collection of vintage wooden oxen. Spanish Revival iron sconces flank fireplace above, Monterey occasional table right, Catalina flowerpot and Monterey holder left.

Detail of faux-wood concrete work topping oversized river rock fireplace.

Detail of vintage Spanish Revival banded iron chandelier, c1930s, one of a pair.

Monterey library table in old wood finish with iron cross bars centers large paned picture window and frames the view of garden and mountains. Catalina Island bright yellow bulbous vases and Cowboy hat in blue sit on a small Mexican saltillo, and share space with a pair of contemporary wrought iron candelabra.

Monterey prohibition bar (branded "Monterey") in medium brown finish with wild bucking bull painting in "Juan Intenoche" style (not signed by artist), stocked with variety of exotic tequilas. Gladding McBean mugs and Catalina server, Catalina Toyon red oil jar in original iron stand c1930 on right.

Detail of whimsical cartoon painting style called "Juan Intenoche" that is sometimes found on Monterey furniture. Wild red bucking bull, cacti, a rider with large moustache and flying sombrero, and Mexican folk florals are favorite themes. Some of these paintings are artist signed, some not. The same artist (whose actual name is unknown) moonlighted for Coronado Furniture as well.

Monterey bookcase with painted interior and old wood exterior showing ample display area for books or collectibles. From the top, Catalina mini oil jar with triple candelabra in Toyon, scout lamp with metal shade in Descanso green, two-handled vase and bulbous vase in Toyon, and wooden box. Monterey table lamp with iron legs and arch, painted sides, and Catalina vase in green on wood tabletop.

Natural light from the tall paned window in great room falls on California plein air painting by A.W. Johnston and comfortable snack table. Table and gold upholstered chairs with old wood finish by Monterey.

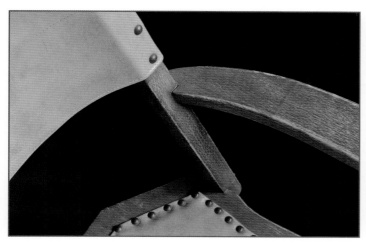

Close-up of a Monterey chair with gold leather back and seat, providing modern appeal and comfortable design.

Stencil painting on ceiling beams found on early California Revival homes descended from European folk art roots. The painted beams add rich detail and the colors can provide a decorating template for complimentary furnishings and textiles.

Detail shows floral painting on Monterey "banana" legged coffee table in multiple colors with a crackle finish.

Detail shows one of several unique stained glass panes embedded in a large leaded glass window original to the home. This pane depicts a lovely señorita being serenaded, c1920s.

Vintage Batchelder pierced tile planter in a sunny niche brimming with tropicals, succulents, and vines.

Close up of twisted hand wrought iron stair rungs and rail.

Understated staircase with double arched inside window at side and top imparts a golden glow. Hand wrought ironwork on stairs is original to the home as are the magnesite steps. Magnesite is a cement-like construction material compounded of magnesium. Artist Noguchi uses magnesite for his sculptures.

Kitchenette in "Playhouse" follows classic tile pattern using contemporary materials in the vintage style.

Opposite page top:
Long, built-in, heavy wood bar in great room. On top sits Catalina Island Descanso green ringed planter, pitcher, tumblers, and tray in turquoise and yellow glazes. Monterey side chair in old brown with iron detail c1930 sits next to vintage Native American rug. Alcove behind bar provides lighting for mural by Taylor Tilery of Indian scout on the plains, c1930.

Opposite page bottom:
Close-up of mural by Taylor Tilery of Indian scout on the plains, c1930.

Roomy bathroom shower has cheerful contemporary yellow and tan 4" tiles inside in a checkerboard pattern and scrolling border in yellow and blue. Solid blue 6" tiles frame the entrance in a nod to the period.

Detail showing subtle yellow and tan tiles with scroll border design and complimentary blue tile. Contemporary tile boasts vintage design.

Tucked into a charming spot, box hedges are formed into diamond shapes linked together like a chain. Vintage concrete birdbath sits at center. Box hedges are often used in California gardens for interest and as borders for definition..

One of many exceptional hardscape and garden treatments found on this property. Here textured concrete pieces were formed to create a driveway surface. Utilizing a large six- pointed star in a circle design, randomly shaped pieces move outward with grass growing in the gaps. A similar "mosaic" treatment is found in the courtyard of the Adamson House Museum in Malibu.

San Marino—
Simple and Austere by
Marston, Van Pelt & Maybury

This fine Spanish Colonial Revival home was built in 1926 and is located in a showcase neighborhood with designs by many notables of the period, including Paul Williams, Reginald Johnson, George Washington Smith, and the designers of this home, Marston, Van Pelt and Maybury. An entire development of speculative homes designed by noted architect Wallace Neff, which includes a 10,000 square foot Mediterranean style villa, said to be designed for the Singer Family, are to be found on the surrounding streets.

The exterior of this two-story home reflects the sedate architecture of southern Spain. Small windows, a simple roofline, and little exterior ornamentation bestow the house with an elegant simplicity, with the exception of a Churrigueresque (or Spanish baroque style) doorway surround. Made for family living, the interior has multiple bedrooms upstairs, and living areas downstairs that include a formal, yet open, dining room, butler's pantry, maid's room, a sweeping spiral staircase, and a user-friendly floor plan that still seems fresh. The gardens surrounding the home continue the California Revival theme by incorporating Mediterranean plants, decomposed granite, and pottery from California's early pottery makers creating a Santa Barbara-like complement to the home's white walls and red-tiled roof.

San Marino is situated fifteen minutes from downtown Los Angeles, near the base of the San Gabriel Mountains, next door to Pasadena. It was originally part of the property associated with the San Gabriel mission, fourth in the California Mission chain and founded in 1771. It is home to the world famous Huntington Library, Art Collections, and Botanical Gardens, a 150-acre non-profit research and educational center that is set amidst breathtaking gardens and was opened to the public in 1928 by Henry E. Huntington. The California Institute of Technology, commonly known as Caltech, has its 22-acre campus here with many buildings designed in the Spanish Revival and Mediterranean style by Bertram G. Goodhue in 1917. San Marino is also home to El Molino Viejo, The Old Mill, built in 1816 as a grain mill for the nearby Mission. It is generally believed to be one of the oldest commercial buildings in Southern California.

The home's original owner was the creator and author of the Charlie Chan detective novels. Earl Derr Biggers wrote five of his novels in the home including *The Chinese Parrot, Behind That Curtain, The Black Camel, Charlie Chan Carries On*, and *Keeper of the Keys.*

The current owners are the third family to live in the well-preserved home adorned with the architect's original doors, hardware, cabinets, flooring and fixtures, which they have kept authentic, yet alive. The house is furnished with an eclectic mix of antiques that reflects their casual lifestyle, their studious appreciation for California's history, and their extensive travels. Spanish, California Revival, Monterey and Asian furniture are situated in comfortable and informal arrangements. California pottery from Bauer and Catalina, tile murals from the San Jose Workshop and Taylor Tilery add splashes of color and share space with historic California plein-air paintings in muted tones. The end result is a simple elegance that also allows for a family friendly environment.

HENRY E. HUNTINGTON LIBRARY & ART GALLERY, SAN MARINO, CALIFORNIA

Vintage postcard from the Huntington Library and Art Gallery.

Entry of an authentic California Spanish Revival home. Oversized wood paneled door painted Spanish green. Molded concrete surround in flower and grape motif.

Detail shot of molded concrete in Spanish Baroque style surrounding front door.

Detail of handmade bronze hardware with unique parrot head handle.

Several breezeways, strategically placed in stucco walls, surround the home and garden areas using Moroccan style concrete blocks stacked in an appealing pattern. Bauer terracotta Indian pot sits atop a wall with a cutaway space filled with stacked terracotta cylinders that allow air circulation and see-through views.

Entry showcases a Monterey buffet in old wood finish topped by a contemporary gold accent mirror. Bauer baby oil jar and strawberry pot in cobalt and orange glazes. Spanish Revival period iron wall sconces.

Iron stair rail curves into light provided by a strategically placed window. Tongue and groove flooring is original. Creamy ivory stucco walls and dark wood accents create an inviting ambience. Vintage Taylor Tilery flying parrot mural. Monterey library table with iron stretchers rests at foot of stairway. Large Bauer oil jar glazed deep orange.

Detail of top of Monterey library table in desert dust finish with hand painted florals.

Heavy original ceiling beams are an important feature of this living room. Built in shelving on either side of fireplace displays collection of mission-themed paintings. Spanish Colonial carved wooden candlesticks on hearth with large Bauer Hilton pot in delft blue. Monterey club chair and arts & crafts Morris chair upholstered in chocolate brown leather. Mission scene depicted on tile table with iron base by Taylor Tilery.

View from living room into entry and stairwell, and thick mission archway to dining room shows the ease and livability of the original design. Plein aire period paintings grace either side of the passageway. Small rectangular Monterey table with iron stretchers. Simple Monterey wood chair with tacked leather seat at entrance to dining area.

Spanish Colonial library table stands under a large wood framed window, featuring twisted iron "branches" with hand formed iron flowers and leaves. Ornate carvings on edges and drawers stained in gold and brown. Low wooden bowl holds vintage wooden bocce balls. Contemporary fabric draperies in rich red and gold repeating floral pattern compliment creamy walls and neutral straw colored carpet.

Close view of plein aire oil painting by important 1930s California artist Edgar Payne in gilt frame. Catalina Toyon red ball lamp with contemporary hand painted shade and Coronado scalloped metal desk lamp sits on Monterey table. Most pottery companies of the era made whimsical cowboy hats in a variety of colored glazes: four are shown here. Elaborate iron ventilation grates were typical for homes of this era, as were the beautifully crafted matching iron sconces with parchment half shades.

Monterey mini-bar sides and top fold and close to disguise it as a small cabinet, a useful feature during prohibition times. Clad copper top prevents water staining. Shelves provide display area for small Bauer Indian pots and cowboy hat, Catalina Island blue Cat-o-Lina whimsical pottery cat with planter opening for a real cactus "tail."

Six-sided old wood finish Monterey gaming table with iron straps and supports with Bauer baby oil jar in cobalt blue. Tile mural was made by one of the San Jose Workshops in San Antonio, Texas during the 1930s. These high quality and brilliantly colored scenics sometimes found their way to California when brought home by tourists.

Long view of roomy dining room shows seven foot long Monterey trestle table and woven strap side chairs in old wood finish along with tile topped buffet cabinet in old red paint. Original Monterey paintings in green and red frames add a whimsical Mexicana touch. Table sits at an angle for added interest.

San Jose Workshop eight-tile mural is a romantic depiction of a couple taking a stroll under a street lamp. Vintage curly top iron frame.

Close in on Monterey buffet shows off black iron hardware and little floral designs in base corners. Bauer jade green ringed fruit bowl. Leather strap side chair. Hispano tile top (not shown). Whimsical signed Monterey paintings of young couple at courtship, and another of same couple many years later.

Close-up view of six place settings of festive Bauer ringware on Monterey dining room table. Mini serape from Mexico c1920s, used as table runner. Silver service gives a touch of elegance.

Whimsical Monterey painting of Mexican man pushing a stubborn burro uphill. Artist signed paintings, referred to now as "Juan Intenoche's" (not thought to be the artist's real name), were offered for sale with Monterey furniture at Barker Brothers, Hales and other fine furniture stores that carried Monterey across the country. This cartoon artist of Mexican heritage was known for his specialty painting on select pieces of Monterey and Coronado furniture and has not, as of this date, been positively identified. The staff at Mason included talented men and women of Mexican, Anglo, and mixed descent, who also deserve credit, along with George and Frank Mason, for the furniture and accessories that are so prized today.

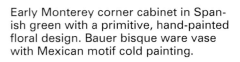

Monterey daybed in Spanish green is perfect fit for small guest bedroom. Primitive floral design on head and footboard, colorful Mexican serape bedcover, and Monterey paintings in original frames.

Early Monterey corner cabinet in Spanish green with a primitive, hand-painted floral design. Bauer bisque ware vase with Mexican motif cold painting.

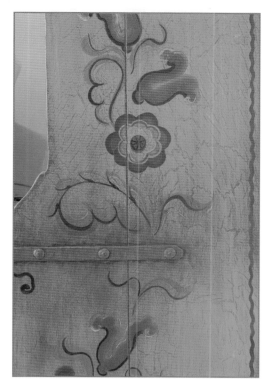

Detail of hand painted florals and crackle paint finish. Hand hammered iron hardware painted orange.

Called the "Will Rogers desk," this is the same found in the historic home of the famed American humorist. It's the largest of the desks made by Monterey, in old wood finish with cutout leather desk chair. Arts & Crafts table lamp and pottery burro accents. Monterey bookcase with extensive hand painted florals. Moroccan design concrete sends shadows though the window.

Simple but striking arrangement of Monterey sofa with inviting chocolate brown leather paired with unusual bright orange D. & M. Chinese dragon-themed tile mural in iron surround.

Vintage orange mesh metal chair rests on bedroom balcony with wooden balustrade. D. & M. tile pot hanger with wrought iron frame holds Bauer Spanish pot. Large Bauer jade green ringed jardinière on the deck could hold magazines or plants. Small circular single tile table with iron base.

Santa Barbara—Elegant Family Living by Reginald Johnson

Santa Barbara is the city that brought Spanish Revival architecture and design into prominence. It is known for the prevalence of its red tile style tradition from its humblest cottage to its Grand Courthouse, as well as the famous Mission Santa Barbara, the queen of the mission chain. San Diego may rightly claim to be the birthplace of the trend, but the world-class designers that brought Spanish Revival to Santa Barbara elevated it into national prominence. Local ordinances even regulate it as the official style of the city.

We are featuring a graceful home in Hope Ranch that was built in 1929, one of the first four originals built in this area designed by master architect Reginald Johnson. His firm, Johnson Kaufmann and Coate, was considered a master of California originated style. Johnson was responsible for many very important buildings in Southern California that sprung up during the Spanish Colonial Revival period from 1915 to 1935, including the influential Santa Barbara Biltmore (now The Four Seasons) and a number of churches including All Saints Episcopal in Pasadena, where, in a pleasing coincidence, our homeowners were married. The church is a landmark building that is listed as part of Pasadena's Civic Center Historic District. The Biltmore caught the eye of many developers and the moneyed class of the day. Reginald Johnson was known among his peers as "the people's architect" because he didn't just design for the upper class, he was a charitable person who was also dedicated to developing design solutions for housing low-income families.

This refined home, like most of Johnson's designs, is eminently livable. The residents of this graceful home love and recognize its classic charm: old world but not stodgy in any way. The layout makes the house easy to navigate and practical to use enabling them to live inside and outside with ease. It's as busy as Grand Central Station—albeit set among ancient oaks—and kids, dogs, cats, and a lizard can all be accommodated. With the exception of a kitchen/family room remodel in the early 1990s the basic "bones" of the home have not been touched and it is in close to original shape with amazing ironwork, heavy stuccowork, beams, arches, courtyards, and all the refined touches of a master architect. Some new custom tile adds a fantastical splash of majesty to the master bath, and faux tile painting around doorways and along walls echo the early traditions of hand craftsmanship that we celebrate. The busy residents of this home call it "the mothership" and with all the activity it effortlessly sustains inside and out we can certainly see why.

Majestic old palm trees, planted in 1904, line the road to this Hope Ranch residence in Santa Barbara, California.

Built in 1929, the understated entry, with lion head stucco and tile fountain, is typical of the subtle elegance found in a Reginald Johnson home.

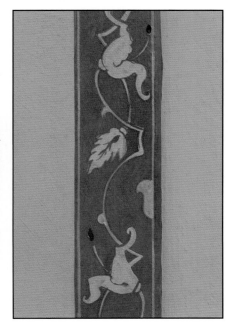

Far left:
Detail shows the front door and walkway to this refined home display detail and symmetry. Iron bench, lighting sconce and screen original to home.

Above:
Detail of superb wrought iron locking screen door.

Left:
Detail of floral border design in blue and white surrounding front door entryway.

Wood beams and white textured ceiling are striking features of this great room. Oversized fireplace has colorful tile surround and border on red tile hearth. Tall wooden mantel with room for collectibles from travels. Two pairs of contemporary velour upholstered club chairs face each other and coordinate with the warm, neutral, palette. Monterey sofa back panels show hand painted florals, with cushions in chocolate colored leather. Monterey coffee table centers the seating area.

Kitchen adjoins the great room and shares the contiguous beamed ceiling. Modern stainless steel appliances include two refrigerators, large range and hood, and in-cabinet warming bins. Stainless covers the large center island. The shiny steel provides contrast to four contemporary wood and leather Monterey style counter seats.

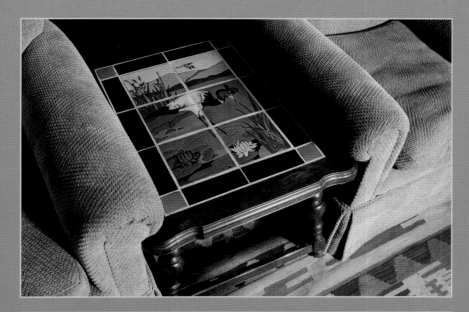

Catalina Island Crested Crane tile table in wooden base, circa 1930s.

Monterey floor lamp with red patina, iron, and folk art flowers boasts a contemporary parchment shade painted to match.

This California Revival style dining area can handle family members and guests with ease. Large Monterey trestle table and majestic chairs, with Catalina Island yellow fruit bowl and Descanso green charger as centerpiece. Vintage Catalina artifacts are displayed between books and collectibles on the built-in bookshelves.

Brightly colored reproduction Catalina tiles border the oversized fireplace with the stylish, detailed wrought iron screen. Some California Revivalists prefer to use reproduction tile in permanent home installations.

Detail of reproduction Catalina Island patterned tiles used on fireplace surround.

Detail showing hand hammering and ironwork on contemporary fireplace screen.

Echoing the home's original design, a bar was carved out next to the formal living room. Elegant Spanish style cabinetry, contemporary field tile backsplash, copper countertops, and wrought iron lighting focus attention on the vintage tile galleon mural by Gladding Mc Bean, c1930s.

Ultimate luxury and tile style in the master bathroom. Undersea Mermaid spa niche was custom made by the contemporary tile makers famous for the Catalina Island's Casino mermaid mural and many other installations. Complimentary field tiles were made to match, as were the two Catalina-style tile designs on pillars entering step-down bathing area with overhead shower.

Hand turned wooden details on glass doors open to flagstone courtyard patio. Contemporary patio furniture and umbrellas invite relaxation. Many doors open onto this central patio and provide easy outdoor access. A large, Catalina Island Pottery, two-handled floor vase, in Descanso green to the right. Vintage California pottery is nestled throughout the grounds.

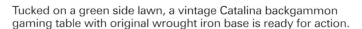

Tucked on a green side lawn, a vintage Catalina backgammon gaming table with original wrought iron base is ready for action.

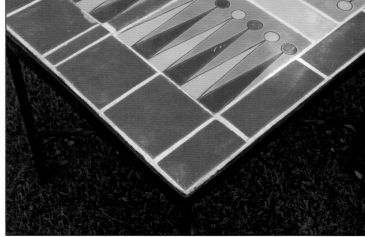

Close-up of Catalina gaming table in aqua and yellow glazes with 8" backgammon tiles shows excellent condition for tiles dating from the early 1930s.

Pasadena Environs—
Spanish Antiquities & Cacti

Built in 1932 in a neighborhood of Spanish Revival residences that were developed for the artsy set, this well-built home boasts a spectacular and award winning garden that is both eye-catching and drought tolerant. The garden is filled with rare cacti and succulents that come from as near as Mexico and as far away as Madagascar.

Pasadena and its neighboring communities of Glendale, Eagle Rock, and others are located in the San Gabriel Valley and were connected by the famous Route 66 all the way to the coast. Pasadena is famous as the birthplace of the Arts and Crafts movement in the United States. The Gamble House is to be found here, an international landmark of California Craftsman style. Charles Lummis, the father of the Arroyo Seco movement, and his home, "El Alisal, the Place of the Sycamore," is now the headquarters of the Historical Society of Southern California. The Arroyo Seco Canyon is a scenic treasure of sylvan glens and sparkling brooks where many California plein air artists lived, thrived, and painted. The Arroyo Seco movement gave rise to successful enterprises, including furniture design and manufacturing, home plans and kits, ceramics, glasswork, metalwork, and textiles, and in many cases provided the artists and the artistic springboard for the creative outpourings of the Spanish Revival to come. More is becoming known everyday about the connection between Arts and Crafts and Spanish Revival, as many architects and artists participated in both movements.

Pasadena is also home to the Rose Bowl Stadium, the world-famous Rose Parade, and the revitalized "Old Town" which includes the Pasadena Playhouse. One can also find and explore the Norton Simon Museum and the Pasadena Museum of California Art.

The decor of this lovely vintage home has a strong emphasis on Spanish Colonial furniture and includes Monterey furniture in a combination that blends well with California art

pottery and tile. Heavy, hewn wooden beams, hard wood and tile floors, neutral walls, and archways make for a traditional old-world feel and provide the perfect backdrop for display. The home is unaltered and its very large backyard is filled with exotic tropical foliage and has a large swimming pool.

This homeowner is an expert in Monterey furnishings, Spanish Revival decor, early California paintings, and has a specialty shop that caters to finding unique pieces for Spanish style homes.

Award-winning cactus garden fronts this classic Spanish Revival home built in 1932. Original thick stucco walls, wrought iron window grates, dark wood doors, and tile roofing.

Wrought iron decorates the peephole of a heavy wooden entry door decorated with a hand-stenciled design. Finely detailed period bronze hardware.

Spanish Colonial furnishings include an intricately carved 16th-17th century vargueno, used as a traveling chest for documents and valuables, shown with 17th century chair with classic accents; heavy carving, leather, and large brass tacks. Spanish señorita painting by California artist Oscar Theodore Jackman (1878-1940).

Detail of colorful Mexican tiles atop iron-based table in living room illustrates the unevenness of hand-made tiles and the use of naive Mexican floral designs.

Right:
Vintage Talavera Mexican vase sits atop a large Mexican tile table with iron base. A hand-wrought candelabrum stands next to an arched niche that provides shelving for favorite objects.

Molded cement fireplace and mantel is accented by elegant iron and mica fire screen adorned with two griffins. California artist Theodore Jackman (1878-1940) oil painting features a señorita flamenco dancer. Decorating the mantel are four round California tiles and a pair of Spanish Revival iron candelabra. On the wall an iron sconce with hide shades salvaged from architect Wallace Neff's estate.

The graceful dining room is tastefully decorated with a Monterey dining table and chairs, iron touches in the chandelier and candelabra, and a contemporary Guatemalan table runner. The pass-through draws the eye towards the kitchen and breakfast nook.

Starburst pattern Monterey buffet topped with bronze-base lamp, c1920s. Staircase boasts twisted iron balusters in an alternating pattern. Iron and wood-beamed ceiling are original to the home. Early 1930s print advertising for the Rose Parade held annually in Pasadena, California hangs at landing next to freestanding candelabra.

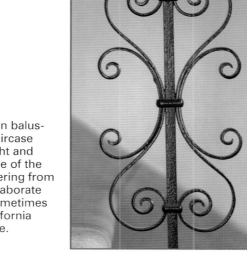

Detail of iron baluster from staircase shows a light and simpler style of the period, differing from the more elaborate versions sometimes seen in California Revival style.

Detail of pressed-cement stair riser that creates a faux tile design.

Right:
Vintage bathroom tile in an eye-catching wainscoting with thin black trim. Porcelain pedestal sink contrasts with intricate ironwork period mirror. Monterey vanity leather topped bench. Lacy iron plant holder suspends three Bauer flowerpots.

San Fernando Valley— Oranges and Roses

When Bing Crosby crooned in the 1940s about making the San Fernando Valley his home, horse and all, it had long been the country getaway for many in the movie business. This home is reminiscent of that earlier time when California homes were both elegant and rustic, when gardens were arranged as outdoor rooms that extended the interior living spaces and when the colors, orange, yellow, green, and blue provided panache to otherwise austere mission-inspired surroundings.

Home to over two million people and commonly known as simply "The Valley," the San Fernando Valley is one of the best-known symbols of suburbia and lies just outside the L.A. basin. It was the hotbed of pre-war ranch style design and developers turned wheat and bean fields into tract homes to meet the needs of the GI's returning from World War II. It doesn't take "val-speak" to make it feel like a favorite neighborhood from your childhood and its familiarity might owe something to the fact that it was also the setting for the movie "E.T." and "The Brady Bunch" television series.

The current owners are the third residents in this home, which dates to about 1930. Quaintness, history, and lavish gardens create a fun blend, and one wouldn't be surprised if a flamenco dancer appeared in the den. Vintage and reproduction California tiles are featured throughout the home along with etched mahogany doors and built-ins. There co-exists a combination of Arts and Crafts era Mission and "Old Wood" and "Old Red" finished Monterey furniture, and Mexicana, Bauer, and Catalina Island Pottery with an emphasis on museum quality historic pieces.

The dance metaphor isn't entirely an invention. The current residents found their dream home when they were invited over one afternoon by their elderly neighbor. In her youth Lelia Goldoni danced with Alvin Ailey, became a featured dancer with the famed Lester Horton Dance Theatre in Los Angeles, and in 1957 made her screen debut in John Cassavetes' ground-breaking film *Shadows*. When they entered the living room, they were awe struck by the massive hand-hewn trussed ceiling, which according to neighborhood legend, were salvaged from the old San Fernando Mission. When the house eventually came up for sale they were waiting.

The original condition of the interiors has remained largely untouched, other than replacing the family room floor, enlarging the kitchen to bring it back in line with the original spirit that had been marred by a 1950s remodel, and adding a custom-tiled swimming pool to the backyard.

The owner, an architect, had realized for some time that the colorful tiles that dotted the cityscape were a

related art form. He began researching the companies responsible for their production and is the co-editor of a series of books on the subject, as well as a lecturer, a frequent contributor to antique journals, and a tile historian. It is a constant pleasure for the owners to live surrounded by the colorful hand-made objects from California's recent past, by the serenity and beauty of their gardens, and by the companionship of their pets. At home with three Siamese cats, two Samoyeds, and, in the backyard, both an aviary and greenhouse full of orchids, visitors often feel like they've been transported to an oasis in what once was a desert.

Inviting fruit trees line the rose-covered entry. A brick pathway transitions to the tile paver landing leading to this 1930s home. Dark stained and paneled door with recent custom wrought iron speakeasy opening, stark white stucco, crisp red tile roofline, giant terracotta strawberry planter, and iron Arts & Crafts drop fixture create perfect symmetry.

Romantic scrolled and floral wrought iron front garden gate and a recently installed colorful vintage tile shard walkway.

Formal living room with off white walls and dark stained wood plank floors keep the room bright and show off the owners' collection of California pottery, tile, and furnishings. Dark heavy beamed ceiling with vintage iron chandeliers. Two Monterey sofas, one with flip up shelf (in foreground) in old brown, both with dark brown leather cushions and floral painted back panels. Vintage Malibu tile table in foreground.

Hand plastered fireplace and mantel with vintage tile trim by Markoff Tile, Inglewood California (1926-45). Catalina Island six-tile green parrot mural in iron frame. Catalina triple candelabra in Descanso green. Rebekah floor vase by Matt Carlton for Bauer in green glaze used for large planter on hearth. Period wrought iron sconces illuminate intricate Moorish design on Catalina Island plates flanking chimney. Taylor Spanish caballero tile c1930.

Entry hall with Moroccan punched metal and colored glass design hanging lamp. Pair of Claycraft tile sconces with mission scenes c1921-39 with contemporary bell motif frames. Iron mirror over old wood finish Monterey tile top buffet. Garden City column vases in a variety of sizes and colors atop buffet. Navajo rug c1930s.

Catalina raised design flare bowl in period iron holder with matching blue pelican flower frog at center and a handled candleholder atop a cabinet. Pressed and unglazed parrot design tile on stand.

Collection of Catalina Island pieces in the study includes a Monterey brown swordfish plate, Descanso green step vase, kissing parrots on black glaze plate, and underwater garden scene on Toyon red bordered plate. Contemporary Arts & Crafts style display cabinet has been wired for lighting.

Dining room features grand chandelier rescued from a local salvage shop composed of wrought iron, stenciled mica panels, and period tile. Dining table set is a family heirloom topped by colorful dinnerware by Metlox. High clerestory window provides additional lighting glow.

Close view of historical wrought iron, heraldic stenciled mica, and tile chandelier is one of several sets of candelabra in the home on which Malibu or Hispano Moresque tile was placed evenly around the outside of the fixture.

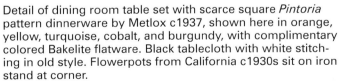

Detail of dining room table set with scarce square *Pintoria* pattern dinnerware by Metlox c1937, shown here in orange, yellow, turquoise, cobalt, and burgundy, with complimentary colored Bakelite flatware. Black tablecloth with white stitching in old style. Flowerpots from California c1930s sit on iron stand at corner.

Manufactured by Cellini Craft, this hammered aluminum and California tile tray and casserole look as good as when first made in 1940s. Antique family heirloom table with vintage parrot motif linen runner.

Sitting room shows blend of Monterey and Arts and Crafts furnishings. Period settle and chair in Stickley-style with red leather cushions and pillows both vintage and new. Monterey corner cabinet in old red finish filled with colorful California pottery, c1920s-30s. Two Catalina Island six-sided tables serve as coffee tables. Early Navajo pastel on mantel is family heirloom. Dried chili pepper ristra hangs on chimney.

An assortment of authentic California vintage tile and shards were added to this fireplace hearth with eye-catching results. Antique andirons are hand-forged iron.

Vintage stylized crackle painting of a Mexican man with pottery by A. Ruelle, c1930-40.

Small tile top worktable with solid color Catalina tile and Monterey painted, rush seat chair. A vintage crackle painting of a Mexican man hangs over the desk, with Bauer server in iron holder and ringed tumblers.

Built in niche with cabinetry shows off two Catalina Island tile bird murals with Gladding McBean wine bottle in Indian form. Top shelf has Catalina Spanish galleon plate, a green deco Indian vase, and large Malibu Moorish plate executed in heavy cuenca style. Catalina ringed flower vase in original wooden stand. Original Arts & Crafts hanging lantern illuminates alcove. Hand painted doorway arches executed by the owner with stencils patterned after Catalina Island tile designs.

Hand painted wood mirror by Coronado Furniture reflects Mexican iron cross candleholder, old Mexican saltillo, Native American basket, and multi-colored votive candleholders made by Catalina Island Pottery.

Large vintage wrought iron mirror with D. & M. tile border placed over Monterey writing desk with leather center and Catalina tile trim, crackle drawer with floral. Catalina Island monument lamp in Descanso green. Matt Carlton floor vase in orange glaze for Bauer Pottery.

Monterey lean-on bar with crackle painted panel featuring Intenoche-style red horse and rider in action, heavy iron foot rail. Terracotta paver floor with reproduction depression-glazed Catalina tile interspersed.

Monterey Bar in old red finish opened to show great painting of Mexican bucking bull rider and florals in Juan Intenoche-style. A variety of California oil jars surround the bar from left, Catalina in Toyon red, right are Garden City and Bauer Pottery glazed orange.

Kitchen was remodeled to feature the owner's collection and to bring it up to par with the vintage character of the rest of the home. Monterey style kitchen cabinets with glass doors keep vintage California pottery safe yet seen. Countertops were replaced with a combination of wood and vintage tile sets by D. & M. and Tudor. Contemporary yellow field tiles were ordered from Mexico. Period tile aquarium in foreground made of vintage Malibu tile.

Refurbished period stove tucks into Mexican yellow tile alcove with vintage Tudor bird mural installation. Hand made wavy edge flowerpots by Matt Carlton for Bauer line top ledge.

Detail of Monterey style curved bottom custom cabinetry and original D. & M. tile set installation in countertop. Garden City bean pots and canisters on counter. Pacific Pottery blended glaze bowls top cabinetry.

Left:
Kitchen bay has built-in seating with focus on round, period Malibu tile table. Wrought iron chandelier is French c1920.

Detail of Malibu tile tabletop showing rich glazes and attention to craftsmanship that was its hallmark.

This tall, period wall fountain was salvaged and put to a new purpose. It features Batchelder dolphin fountain piece and American Encaustic tiles in deco design.

Beverly Hills— Movie Stars and Starry Nights

Most people hear Beverly Hills and think high-end shopping and ostentatious wealth. California Revival collectors think vintage Spanish homes, some jewel boxes and others sprawling mansions by well-known architects such as Wallace Neff, Reginald Johnson, and George Washington Smith.

This home is situated in a secluded part of Beverly Hills that most people don't know exists. In 1828 the Valdez family first settled here and named the area "Rodeo de las Aquas" translated as the "Gathering of the Waters" because of the underground artesian springs that ran down from the foothills. The Beverly Hills Hotel was built at that same site in 1912 and was named after Beverly Farms in Massachusetts. Landscape designer Wilbur D. Cook was heavily influenced by Frederick Law Olmstead and created wide curving streets that hugged the hills. The first streets had Spanish sounding names such as Rodeo, Cañon, Crescent, Carmelita, Elevado, and Lomitas.

Not deterred by the country atmosphere and the sparse amenities, and without a Gucci store in sight, Edward L. Doheny built his hunting lodge in this local canyon around 1918. Soon enough the Beverly Hills Hotel became the center of community life, serving as theater, meeting place, and church, and when many movie stars were attracted to the area it entered a glamorous phase. Douglas Fairbanks and Mary Pickford were among the trendsetters when they built their mansion *Pickfair* there in 1919. Gloria Swanson, Will Rogers, Thomas Ince, Charlie Chaplin, Tom Mix, Ronald Coleman, King Vidor, John Barrymore, Buster Keaton, Harold Lloyd, Jack Warner, Clara Bow, Marion Davies, Harry Cohn, and Rudolph Valentino soon followed and built stylish homes. Rogers, a wise cracking political humorist, became honorary mayor of Beverly Hills and went on to play a part in its development by fostering construction of a new City Hall in 1932 and the establishment of a U.S. Post Office in 1934, before finding out he'd done too good a job. Now that things were bustling, he decided to move out to his Pacific Palisades polo ranch and outfit it with Monterey furniture.

This period Spanish Revival home is situated on a narrow street with vintage streetlights and no sidewalks, and an atmosphere that seems far away from the hustle and bustle of Los Angeles. Keeping up with the movie star tradition, this particular neighborhood became a haven for actresses Fay Wray and Veronica Lake during the 1940s and, more recently, actor Mathew Modine lived in this featured home. After a year of searching, when the new owners walked into this house they knew immediately that it was *the one*. The neighborhood has its own distinct charm and character. Most of the homes are Spanish, but there are also Art Deco,

Vintage postcard shows movie star's Spanish style bungalow.

English Tudor, Mid-Century Modern, Ranch, and English Cottage style homes. A nearby orange grove has stood for over a hundred years and one can see deer nibbling away at the fallen fruit. Many of the homes still sport trees from the original grove in their front yards, which pleases the hummingbirds that flit here and there. The backyard abuts state park land where dogs can play. A variety of wildlife can be seen including a wide assortment of birds, deer, coyotes, opossums, raccoons, even a lynx or two. The canyon is very quiet, and at night the stars shine bright.

Built in 1927 with a traditional courtyard and a lot of windows and light, rare and original Claycraft tiles line the fireplace and are embedded in the stucco courtyard walls.

Most of the home's decor dates back to the 1920s and 1930s, which makes the owners feel like they are entering another era whenever they walk into the house. Vintage Monterey, Coronado, Imperial, and Del Rey, all made in Los Angeles and sporting different finishes and colors, mix and match well. As avid collectors of California tiles for over twenty years they think of them as little pieces of art. Like other collectors of the period, being surrounded by these colorful bits of history makes them happy. Several rooms have their own tile themes: Spanish Galleons, Spanish Dancers, Birds, and California Missions.

A new project is going to be featured as "the Catalina Room." The husband also has a theme room for the extensive baseball memorabilia he's collected since he was a child.

Active preservationists in the Los Angeles area, the owners are concerned when vintage homes are destroyed for the sake of McMansions built up to the property lines. They are surely doing their part in keeping up this immaculate and authentic home as well as pursuing dedicated activities in volunteering, as a museum board member and lecturing on the subject of historic tiles, with an emphasis on historic Malibu tile. As people continue to appreciate the efforts being made in this emerging conservation field, more vintage homes, iron work, tile, craftsmanship, and even cement work is being recognized as being culturally, historically, and artistically important.

The timeless style and superior construction of these 1920-30s residences has allowed their various owners to keep them in almost original condition, as this fine example shows.

Below:
A pure, yet playful interpretation of California Revival style. Stained and paneled heavy wood front door with Malibu star tiles on either side. Vintage iron and mica light fixture with ship design. Hand hooked floral rug on dark stained wood floors.

Close view of lacy iron grate over small window within wood paneled entry door. Malibu star tile to right of door with Persian motif. Period iron and mica hanging lamp with ship design in iron.

Entry hall features impressive 12" D. & M. galleon tile mural with card suit corners, and a Gladding McBean four-tile galleon mural above. The Bauer coffee server with ringware tumblers in iron, and the Catalina Island Toyon Red fluted florist vase on right both sit on interesting vintage iron bases topped with tile. Beyond we see dining room and stairwell.

Comfortable living room attains its serenity from the use of various textures and period furnishings. Monterey wingback chairs in Spanish green and old red with floral decorations in foreground. On walls important Malibu and Catalina ship plaques. Round tile table at right with elaborate wrought iron base and small crescent shaped tile table next to sofa, one of a pair.

Long view living room showing period hand painted galleon hanging panel. Coffee table has iron base and tray top filled with single Malibu border tiles under glass. Coronado sofa with original red vinyl upholstery and Gladding Mc Bean oil jar on hearth. Overhead the dining room opening provides a perfect spot to feature Spanish themed tiles by Malibu Potteries in wrought iron frameworks.

Clean lines and interesting details in this cozy fireplace with terracotta pavers and Claycraft tile trim. Wrought iron half round fire screen is vintage Spanish Revival. Mantel is wrapped in hammered and embossed copper.

Close-up of a selection of Malibu Potteries 6" and smaller border tiles under glass on coffee table.

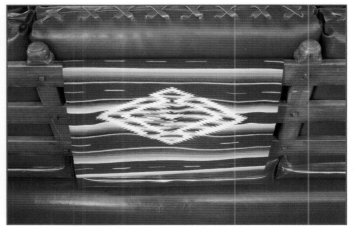

Mexican saltillo blanket graces the Coronado sofa's back in colors complimentary to the red X-stitched original cushions.

Dining area with Monterey table and chairs in medium brown finish. Hand painting and crackle on all with "river of life" design around table skirt. Imperial Furniture Company sideboard topped with Malibu tile at back wall holds Monterey yellow-gold turned wooden lamp. Tile murals above sideboard by Taylor Tilery.

Close in on tile in sideboard by Imperial Furniture Company, c1930s, shows three recessed Malibu tile panels. Monterey yellow-gold wooden table lamp with contemporary shade hand painted to match, and artist painted Catalina plate of California Mission. Tile mission and Spanish style hotel murals are by Taylor Tilery, Los Angeles California.

Guest bedroom entry sports custom painted Mexicana stenciled and textured walls. The giant maguey plant "grows" over the sombrero dotted faux wainscoting. Spanish themed D. & M. tile mini-mural in contemporary iron at left provides nice asymmetry.

Two-toned Monterey-style hutch features cups, teapot, vases, tiles and candleholders from some of the best California potteries: Catalina Island, Pacific Pottery, Gladding McBean, Garden City, Bauer, D. & M., and Malibu tile. Large Catalina Island mission scene plate painted in the 1930s. California Mission Bell replicas were made in early 1900s and placed along the roadside of El Camino Real, Highway 101; then, in the 1940s, small collectible replicas were made, as seen atop hutch.

Painted wainscoting continues into the guest bedroom, which has a Monterey vanity with matching mirror and stool in scarce blue color with flamboyant florals. LAMOSA tile with Mexican couple dancing and a fun Monterey table lamp sit on top. Taylor Tilery tile Spanish dancers mural in wood is left.

The guest bathroom, with a profusion of Mexican Talavera tile and hand painting over window, provides a distinctive welcome to guests. Monterey mirror with desert dust finish over basin.

Monterey bedroom ensemble consists of a single bed, dresser, vanity, and mirror and side table in Monterey blue. Vintage saltillo bedspread was chosen for its complimentary colors. Draperies are period woven fabric with Mexicana cactus and sombrero theme. Pillows are embroidered with like images. Iron ceiling fixture, c1925. Single señorita mural over bed by Taylor Tilery. Monterey era iron table lamp on tile table bedside incorporates plant holders.

Close view of two murals by Taylor of señoritas and caballero. Drapes are vintage Mexicana print, which inspired the stenciling on wainscoting. Large pomegranates on glazed plate by a San Jose Workshop above window.

Corner hutch by Del Rey furniture is painted with red flowers on golden yellow crackle. Jade green and orange glazed fan vase by Bauer's Matt Carlton as is the green mini oil jar. Catalina candleholders in Descanso green. Monterey plant stand with bright yellow Bauer Spanish pot and cactus. Little mission mural is Taylor Tilery in earthy tones and matte finish.

Detail of original geometric Claycraft tile installation on patio wall of California Revival décor home.

This inset courtyard wall mural with a bouquet centerpiece tile was created by Claycraft Tile, c1930s, and is one of the many charming and rare features of this original California Revival home. Vintage concrete cactus stand holds birdbath bowl used for succulent display.

Santa Ynez Ranch—
Horses and Vines

The Santa Ynez Valley as long been known as Santa Barbara's wine country, but it has found new fame and popularity since it was featured in the movie *Sideways,* as well as being home to singer Michael Jackson's Neverland Ranch and Ronald and Nancy Reagan's western White House. The valley includes the towns of Solvang, Santa Ynez, Ballard, Buellton, Los Olivos, and Los Alamos. The nearby Mission Santa Inés was named in honor of Saint Agnes, an early Christian martyr. The American Yankees anglicized the spelling and named the town and the valley Santa Ynez. Once here people can take a deep breath and enjoy the open space and beauty of California the way it used to be. The wines in this area have gained international recognition and the history, agriculture, and scenery make this valley a wonderful place to visit or live.

We are featuring this comfortable ranch-style home, which includes a world-class winery and vineyards. This substantial property is nestled in Ballard Canyon surrounded by rolling, oak-studded hills. The house is on a forty-eight acre lot with eighteen acres planted to vines. The adjoining parcels total about six hundred acres. Arabian and Quarter horses are kept nearby and there are numerous trails for the family and guests to enjoy. Part of an original Spanish land grant called "Rancho San Carlos de Jonata," it was originally a simple ranch home built in the 1950s. First owned by Dr. Gene and Rosalie Hallock, the property included an established winery and vineyards that had operated for over twenty-five years. The new owners totally replanted the vineyards in 2001, and the first vintage from Rusack Vineyards new vines was made in 2005. Varietals were chosen that are uniquely suited to the microclimates and include Merlot, Cabernet Franc, Sangiovese, Sauvignon Blanc, Semillion, Syrah, Petit Syrah, and Petit Verdot. The house and the winery buildings were extensively refurbished and renovated by the new residents in 1992.

When considering their remodel the owners felt strongly that the property suited itself to a California Rancho design scheme, sometimes called Hacienda style. They were desirous of a home with easy access to the outdoors, open beam ceilings and both window and wall space for their western-influenced art collection as well as the wonderful pieces of Monterey furniture they had acquired over the years. They sought to recreate Catalina tile motifs in the kitchen, fireplace surround, and entry, and to showcase important pieces of historic California tile and pottery. After studying and photographing Cliff May's ranch style homes in Sullivan Canyon in Brentwood they even had the opportunity

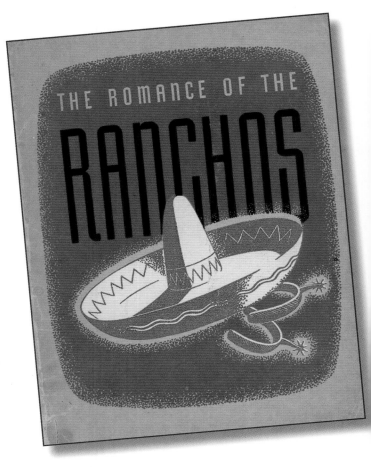

Booklet from 1940s.

to meet with the aging design legend. Incorporating May's use of the "three sidings" approach by using a combination of board and batten, stucco, and adobe, they added a rich exterior look to the dwelling. Heavy red tile roofing added a historically accurate touch and tied all the elements together.

This award winning winery is exceptional for more than just their fine handcrafted wines: it is the only winery to feature a beautiful Catalina tile on its label. To the owners "Catalina tiles have always represented a tradition of hand-crafted excellence and creativity, originated and carried on by a small group of talented people who truly cared about what they did." They chose a Catalina tile to grace their wine label not only because they "love the simple elegance and vibrant colors of these old designs, but also because of Catalina's longstanding importance in our lives." We'll drink to that.

View of wild-flowers and vineyards.

Sprawling one level Hacienda style Ranch home with Spanish tile roof, porches running the length of the home, front and back, with flowers in large terra cotta pots and comfortable outdoor furniture. Rolling grassy lawn and perfect blue-sky finish this transformation from rremodeled 60s ranch to a perfect example of California Revival living.

Green Adirondack chairs sit on long porch area facing vineyard and rose laden view. Catalina Island pottery hanging lamp.

Old Catalina Island pottery hanging lamp created from mixing bowl capped by original hand hammered and decorated metal shade and holder.

Historic, star-patterned tiles bordered by 6" yellow field tile, produced by Catalina Island Pottery, in wrought iron frame and base late 1920s. These tiles were among the first to be produced in the high glaze line possibly concurrent with ceramist Rufus Keeler's ceramic design contributions on the Island. Antecdotal evidence points to Keeler coming Catalina early on as a consultant, perhaps bringing-some of his Malibu designs and glazes with him, in the late 1920s (Kaiser interview). Contemporary iron patio chairs.

Up close view of Catalina Island star tile table, featuring classic 6" tiles from the late 1920s.

Catalina lamp in Descanso green, c1930s, has hand painted seagulls on its replica parchment lampshade. Rare polar bear ashtray with thick white glaze is Catalina Island pottery, aficionados sometimes call him "cubby." Close view of tile topped Monterey buffet by prolific Taylor Tilery Los Angeles California c1920s-30s.

Monterey buffet toped with Taylor Tilery geometric design tiles in old wood. Large Gladding McBean multi-tile Spanish galleon mural in original wood frame on wall, as well as four-tile galleon on buffet. Catalina Island Pottery made the two scout lamps with pottery bases and wrought iron fittings, and the rare bear ashtray in ivory glaze with cold paint facial features (Wrigley's Chicago Cubs baseball team had summer training on Catalina), c1930s. Contemporary hand painted lampshade and Mexican crosses add interest.

Close look at four-tile Gladding McBean ship mural in original wood frame, c1920s-30s. Catalina Island scout lamps with copper shades.

Detail of unusual iron fireplace screen with waves, water, and bubbles theme blends sets off undersea garden tile surround.

Reproduction Catalina Island tile design with Marlin and undersea garden scene surrounds fireplace. Catalina Island pottery seafoam glaze oil jar in original island-made iron holder graces hearth. Contemporary wrought iron fireplace screen and tools were made to compliment the tiles.

Indian basketry goes well with vintage Mexican hand glazed charger and Catalina seafoam trumpet vase filled with roses from the property and bring life to corner shelf.

Large Catalina Island pottery oil jar with rare seafoam glaze in original island-made iron stand c1930s on hearth in corner of living room. Tall Catalina trumpet vase, antique Indian baskets with geometric designs, and colorful hand decorated Mexican charger sit on built in stucco corner shelf.

Bright yellow vintage Catalina Island pottery wine server and plate/tray with small tumblers.

Imperial trestle table with set of four chairs with tacked leather seats, c1930s. A large western style iron light fixture made locally casts a warm glow. Catalina wine pitcher and tray on table with multi colored tumblers and cowboy hat ashtray.

Detail of Imperial trestle dining table and side chairs shows distressed finish and the pointed metal tips that help distinguish it from Monterey furniture. Vintage Native American rug.

George Mason designed Monterey furniture for his father's company, Mason Manufacturing in Los Angeles California, from 1929 to 1943, and during that time they made a handful of grand pianos–less than thirty total. Purchased from an estate in Beverly Hills, anecdotal evidence indicates movie star Rudolph Valentino once owned this one. This rare piece in the old wood finish and traditional floral embellishments. Matching Monterey piano bench with iron stretcher. Vintage Native American rug with reverse swastika, cross, and star design.

Detail photo showing classic Spanish style handcrafted ornamental iron stretchers under Monterey grand piano.

Right:
Detail of old wood finish, old red paint on underside of top and other interior pieces, and floral painting on side of Monterey grand piano.

Close view of
Monterey grand
piano in old
wood finish with
top opened to
show fabulous
old red paint
and simple
floral paintings.
Catalina trum-
pet vase with
flowers, seafoam
glaze.

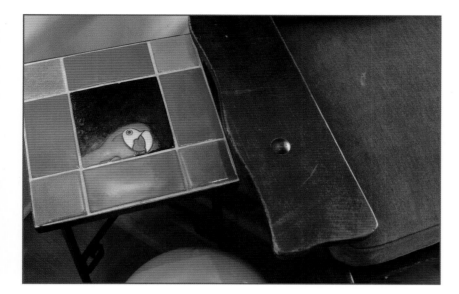

Catalina parrot head tile at center of small iron deco base table by Catalina Island Pottery, c1929, rests next to a Monterey wing-back chair in a dark finish.

Contemporary and intricate compass point circular tile set shown in this table and is repeated in the entry. Vintage Catalina Island ringed planter at center of table.

Sonoma Valley— Redwood and Walnuts

Nestled in the "Valley of the Moon" in northern California, about an hour north of San Francisco, is this newly built contemporary Ranch style home. Sonoma Valley's wine country has a rural flavor with deep agricultural roots as well as world-class wineries, and gourmet and literary credentials. Food writing legend MFK Fisher lived down the road and California author and icon Jack London made his home at the "Beauty Ranch," now a Historic State Park. One of the leading horticulturalists of his day, Luther Burbank, lived and experimented with new plant species in the nearby community of Santa Rosa.

This property lies on the valley floor and was settled in the early 1900s by the Thunberg family, who planted a redwood tree in 1924 that has grown to a stately height of over a hundred feet. Walnut trees planted in the 1950s still produce today. The current residents are the second owners of the obsidian flaked property where native Americans used to work their arrowheads and gaze up at Sugarloaf Ridge, now a protected state park and part of the Mayacamas mountain range that separates the Sonoma and Napa Valleys. With a peak that rises up to 2,729 feet, a few hours hiking on a clear day provides a view that includes both valleys, portions of the San Francisco Bay and even a glimpse of the Sierra Nevada.

The Sonoma Valley is known for warm inland days with evenings cooled by the nearby coast, and boasts a casual outdoor lifestyle where boots come off at the door. This custom home was built in 2004 with a board and batten exterior echoing the historic barns and water towers in the area. Its design themes incorporate the regional vernacular, utilizing low slung ranch styling,

Vintage postcard of the Sonoma Mission, northernmost in the California Mission chain.

metal corrugated porch roofing, sage coloring exterior, and redwood accents. Repeating themes include rectangles, silver metal accents, and the use of the colors red and green. The architectural forms are straightforward with clean lines. Using both neutral and modern interior treatments, the California Revival styling is accomplished purely through accessorizing.

Ranch style homes follow California Revival's traditions from the earliest Spanish Ranchos to Clifford May's 1950s designs, and traces of 1960s modern. Intended to take advantage of California's weather, these homes were designed for the indoor and outdoor lifestyle that brought the patio culture into life and ironically also helped fuel the 1930s taste in brightly colored dinnerware. Expansive use of glass and exterior doors in almost every room brings the outdoors in and allows for access to nature, light, and a casual style.

Playful Mexican colors compliment the neutrality of walls and furniture, while both the romantic and whimsical nature of the style and themes are allowed free rein. The owner is an avid collector of Catalina and California tile and pottery and actively promotes its awareness, pursues research, and has a business devoted to helping other collectors find their dream pieces.

Being both a dealer and a collector poses its challenges, she calls her decorating style, "curatorial." With a constantly changing inventory coming in and going out of the home, the family lovingly calls it the "rotating display."

California Revival is a perfect compliment to the Ranch style home whether older or newly built and is versatile enough to encompass your particular collecting passions and tastes whether Spanish, Mexican, Rancho, or a mixture of all three.

Vintage postcard shows California Redwoods in Northern California.

Mission Arts & Crafts, one of the San Jose Workshops, created this scenic serenade mural with original iron plant motif framework, which is the focal point of this entry hall. Monterey Deco bar in Desert Dust finish with flowers and a metal footrest. Pottery display includes Garden City flowerpots in mural holders, Bauer oil jars on floor and topping divider wall, Catalina Island examples on bar top and their Moorish plates on wall.

Historic tile slabs recovered from the original Catalina Country Club patio on Avalon, now repurposed as garden steps. Early Catalina depression-glazed tiles and bricks were among the first items made by the Catalina Clay Products Company in 1928.

Ranch style home is a custom contemporary design that blends in with the local historic farm structures. Board and batten exterior with modern entry treatment features clear glass doors. Two San Jose Workshops tile murals depict stylized agaves, standing pair of Catalina Island cobalt blue oil jars, a pair of Gladding McBean turquoise urns, and two large vintage Hillside pottery shard pots flank entry. Gus the ranch dog on the porch, which features corrugated metal roof overhang and redwood beam accents.

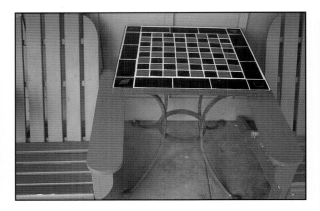

Catalina checkerboard table flanked by red wooden porch chairs. (*Photo courtesy of Robert Benson.*)

Detail of Hillside-Bauer pottery shard planter with early Catalina hand coiled oil jar in cobalt glaze, Gladding McBean turquoise urn planter with two small concrete and Claycraft tile cube planters, all vintage California, 1920-30s.

Old red historic farm buildings
seen through the redwood trees.
(*Photo courtesy of Robert Benson.*)

Unusual Monterey Deco bookcase in Desert Dust finish,
with shelves and bottom compartment door in crackle and
floral, iron pull. Monterey mirror with elaborate Mexican style
florals and orange trim. Bauer hand thrown cactus pots on
bottom shelf, Catalina tray and vase on second shelf. Mexicana metalwork and wooden cactus grouping sits on top.
Monterey-style wooden divider screen with primitive floral
painting and crosshatched design.

Detail of bar top shows a Catalina Island Pottery cactus bowl
filled with cactus shaped salt & peppershakers in variety of
glazes, Toyon red mini oil jar and raised design water jug.
Garden City flowerpot in iron hanger. Catalina Moorish plate
in yellow and black glazes measures 11" across.

Modern high ceiling and clean lines feature in this Great Room, designed as a neutral backdrop for the owners' collections. Two early Monterey club chairs in foreground with rope bases and floral backs, provide comfy seating; a tall Santa Monica Brick patchwork tile table with scroll iron base stands between them. Contemporary leather sofa with vintage Navaho blanket and round Tudor tile shard coffee table. Tabletops feature Catalina Island pottery selections mainly in Descanso Green glaze. California plein aire oil painting by Bud Upton (1900-1988), c1940s, on mantel. Upton was an important Catalina Island Pottery artist and was also responsible for creating some of Catalina's most popular novelties such as the *Siesta Man* ashtray. Large period mural on board with a romanticized Spanish flare, artist unknown. Pair of vintage wrought iron floor candelabra on sides of fireplace, Asian patterned rug.

Close view of Descanso green grouping of Catalina Island pottery on Tudor tile top table made of 4" tiles in green and orange pattern.

Great Room through wide-angle lens shows kitchen on the right. Fireplace wall separates the room from entry but leaves open flow of light and space for views inside and out. Tall and ornate iron base table with Tudor tile top, c1930s, sits under period California Revival mural.

Fireplace mantel created out of a heavy redwood beam with small vintage Malibu border tiles underneath. California plein aire oil painting, *Sycamore Canyon*, by Roger "Bud" Upton, c1940s. Catalina Island pottery cactus flasks in Descanso green, original ivy design iron potholder and pot with cacti, and two types of Indian vase. Iron candelabra, c1920s. Bauer oil jars in cobalt, yellow, green, and turquoise on wall top.

Close-up of vintage Malibu border tiles on fireplace. Contemporary terra cotta pavers are used for entry floor and matching fireplace surround.

Catalina pitcher and cups in original iron holder on colorful Tudor tile coffee table with original iron base. Older Asian carpet covers the thick wood floor. Vintage hand painted Bauer bisque ware with cactus and Mexicana motif in background.

Detail of tabletop by the Imperial
Cabinet Company, L.A., which they
inset with a six-sided tile set made
by the Malibu potteries, c1927.

California orchid cactus oil painting, c1930s, unsigned. Catalina
Island pottery black cactus tail
planter, called a *Lina* (as in Cat
o' Lina), three mini oil jars and
ringed lamp in Toyon red with
original hand painted shade,
large Toyon ringed planter in
original island-made wood
holder. Tall Imperial wooden
table with turned wooden legs,
iron, and vintage Malibu Potteries tile top.

Wide view of the modern kitchen with vintage touches. O'Keefe and Merritt stove from the 1950s is topped by a modern vent hood with stainless steel tile backsplash and appliances. Cherry cabinetry, modern lighting, neutral counter tile, contemporary wine country watercolors, and a bountiful display of vintage California pottery.

Designed as a focal point for the room, the owner's vintage stove does double duty for cooking and display. Modern vent hood, stainless steel subway tiles provide a modern touch to the backsplash. Bauer stacked refrigerator jars, ringed syrup pitchers, large sugar shaker, round butter, and orange glazed cookie jar. San Jose Workshop decorative plates on wall.

Festive table set with hard to find Brayton Laguna pottery dinnerware and accessories, made in Laguna Beach from the 1920s to the 1940s. Mini Mexican saltillo with silk fringe used as table runner. Monterey style three-panel wood screen with floral and crackle painting.

Stainless steel worktables in airy kitchen reflect beautiful cobalt blue pottery display. Watercolor paintings by local artist Robert Benson.

Monterey Welsh cupboard with scalloped top, c1930. Old wood finish and dark iron latches. bright Bauer display of mini Indian pots. Top shelf holds the very smallest 3" size, middle shelf shows 5" size. Bauer artist Matt Carlton created the two hand thrown twist handle vases as well as the wavy lipped planter in jade green. Rare Bauer diamond step next to Bauer scout lamp. Richly detailed oil painting of a Mexican man with fighting rooster by listed artist Rudolf Wetterau of New York c1930s.

Detail shot of Bauer selection. Massing similar forms by the same maker gives visual impact. Ringed vases in cobalt blue and turquoise, trio of ringed pitchers in cobalt, and large jade green ringed platter, topped by individual plain ware coffee pot and hand thrown mini mugs.

Large Coronado Bar with painting of Mexican man pulling a stubborn horse to water signed by the artist known as "Juan Intenoche" (see *Terminology*) and used to display a collection of Catalina lamps and Bauer pottery in the "Catalina Room." Artist signed Monterey painting hanging above depicts a Mexican man hanging onto a wild horse painted in whimsical cartoon style. Hand painted lamp shades are reproductions of originals done by Catalina artist Maude Chase; one is a pattern reminiscent of vintage Catalina *Memorial* tiles.

Original stone plate litho by graphic artist Otis Shepard, c1930s, shows his interpretation of Avalon, a town on Catalina Island. Shepard was art director for Wrigley Chewing Gum and helped "brand" Avalon in the old California-style at the request of P.K. Wrigley. Imperial corner cabinet with iron latched storage below and open shelves with scalloped borders above. Dark finish on mahogany shows off primary colored Catalina pieces. Catalina oil jars in seafoam green and ivory surround Spanish Green Monterey bookshelf. Catalina Island pottery kissing parrots plate in small 8" size hangs above a framed Descanso green kissing fish tile. On bookshelf is Catalina Toyon ringed flowerpot, their monk bookends, and Gladding McBean single señorita tile.

Spanish green Monterey fold-down writing desk, topped by contemporary oil painting of Birch tree by local artist Bobbette Barnes, invites attention at the end of the hallway. Small cobalt rose bowl in iron holder on desk by Bauer artist Fred Johnson. Another Bauer artist, Matt Carlton created the 20" orange glazed two-handled floor vase, called a Rebekah, as well as the shorter hands on hip-handled vase. A cluster of Bauer oil jars and Indian pots anchor the look.

Oval Monterey Spanish style table with wrought metal stretchers. Malibu monk bookends signed 1927 and hefty round Catalina garden pot in Descanso green. Various examples of Malibu kissing parrots tile and peacock panel, Calco peacock tile, Batchelder advertising ashtray, and a rare salesman's sample box of Malibu tile designs, 1926-32.

Airy neutral bedroom allows a colorful collection of vintage tile to stand out. Tile tables and large iron-framed wall mural are by the San Jose Workshops. Shown with Monterey buffet and end table, Navaho Indian rugs, c1940, Catalina Island pottery. Sepia-toned scenes of rural Mexico taken in the 1920s by photographer Hugo Brehme, recessed halogen lighting, and straw colored carpeting contribute to the room's understated appeal.

San Jose Workshop mural entitled *La Paloma* translated as "The Dove" shows traditional costume on bride. It is composed of 6" tiles and smaller orange borders and a contemporary reproduction iron framework. Heavily painted Monterey buffet drawers with Catalina's crane shaped flower frog with matching bowl, hard-to-find monument lamp, and oil jar, all in Descanso green.

Monterey wood chairs with tacked leather seats in red and brown leather, one with footstool. Mexican vintage saltillo and Indian pattern camp blanket used as throws. Early handled floor vase in bright blue by Catalina Island. Large tile scene table attributed to one of the San Jose Workshops, and Monterey four-tile stand in Spanish Green. Unusual tile mural of Spanish dancers attributed to Taylor Tilery, c1934-38, in contemporary iron frame.

Corner wall features a collection of San Jose Workshop glazed Mexicana scenic plates with brown borders. Wood burning stove uses large and small Catalina Island tile cube planters for wood and kindling storage.

Casual Monterey side chair with orange and floral painted wood arms, brown leather back and seat. Small, Spanish green footstool with brown leather cushion and rope detail. Camp blanket on chair, Monterey wood and iron accent table. Period prayer rug chosen for its complimentary color palette.

Master bath uses white, subway tile walls with slate wainscoting, earthly slate floors, recessed halogen lighting, and stainless accents, creating a contemporary hardscape "frame" to show off the colorful Taylor Tile sailboat and Island-themed mural. Catalina flowerpots top mirror and a large patchwork sampler table uses 6" D. & M. tiles in a replica iron scroll base.

California tile maker D. & M. made this unusually sized pair of Spanish troubadour and dancer tiles in a large vertical format. Metal "T" hangers allow the backs and sides to be accessed for study and identification. Partial San Jose Workshops mural is made of four 6" tiles. Tall S & S tile-topped entry table with reproduction iron base. Bauer Indian pots on floor in jade green (largest size they made), smaller orange version on table.

Hallway features modern halogen track lighting to create a gallery feel for paintings, pottery, and furniture, and leads to a suite of bedrooms.

Another view of bath featuring walk-in spa shower with contemporary acorn tile insert, birch spa mat and bench, and versatile patchwork sampler D. & M. vintage table with shelf.

Period oil painting of Spanish couple by Oscar Theodore Jackman in a cozy guest bedroom with a Western flare. Jackman was a well-known graphic artist and illustrator whose poster prints were used to decorate Monterey displays at Barker Brothers. Monterey leather top table, hand tooled with longhorns and cactus, at window, Catalina Island single tile and iron lamp, their trophy lamp in Descanso green with hand painted shade, and oxcart scenic painted plate. Monterey straw ivory double bed with simple tulip florals on head and footboard. Imperial Gentleman's chest and bedside table, Monterey crackle-painted wagon wheel lamp.

Close view of green Imperial gentleman's chest with hand hammered latches and drawer pulls. Vintage mini pottery in a period children's toy version of a Monterey China cabinet, Monterey crackle-painted wagon wheel lamp. Cold-painted (see *Terminology*) scenic plate of oxcart by Catalina artist Francis Graham shows fine detail. Longhorn cattle figure, attributed to San Jose Workshop.

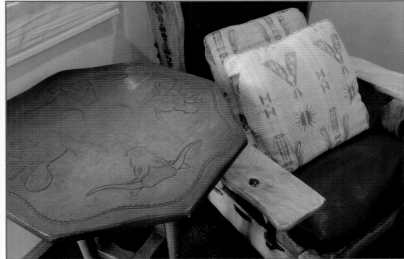

Detail of unusual longhorn and cactus, hand tooled, leather top Monterey table. Straw Ivory finish and early florals on Monterey wing back chair with brown glove leather cushions and vintage Indian motif fabric pillows.

Cartoon-like signed Monterey Mexicana painting on board, with original yellow wood frame. This artist signed "Juan Intenoche" painting is the "after" of a man taking a flower pot to the head. The "before" version show the same man serenading a lady at her window with his guitar. Monterey floor lamp, wood table combination with hand painted metal shade. (*Guitar display courtesy of Jackson Rosenfeld.*)

Rescued from the classic 1920s Spanish style Bakersfield Inn (no longer extant), this historic Batchelder double peacock design wall fountain with Claycraft covered wagon scene tile has found a home in Northern California and awaits a new installation. Batchelder Tile Company, Los Angeles, California, c1909-1932.

Close view of large covered wagon tile, Claycraft Tile, 1921-39.

A vintage Hispano Moresque tile set adorns this large six-sided patio table with matching pattern and border tiles in iron base. Catalina pitcher and señor and señorita salt and peppers for size perspective. Contemporary metal and mesh patio chairs.

Detail of exquisite tile cutwork that carefully matches patterns in the decorative and border tiles in iron framed patio tabletop.

Newport Beach— Elegant and Eclectic on the Bay

Vintage Postcard of the famous "Pottery Shack" on the Pacific Coast Highway.

This Newport Beach harbor view home, designed and built by Orange County realtor-developer John McMonigle in 2000, is in an exclusive area that financier Warren Buffett calls home. We've shown Mediterranean and Italian style homes, Mexican style or Spanish traditional, Ranch, or modern as different frameworks in which to showcase the California Revival elements—to say it's a versatile style that works with many different architectural motifs is an understatement. Here we find an elegant example of the expansiveness and versatility of California Revival that is a completely creative expression of its visionary super-collector owner who seamlessly blends Mediterranean, Spanish and Italian influences while utilizing California Revival as it's major decorative element.

Newport Beach is located in Orange County, a.k.a. "The O.C.," and features many long standing vacation destinations like the Balboa Bay Club, the Festival of Lights, the Laguna Arts Festival, the Balboa Fun Zone, and of course Disneyland. This area was once largely part of the historic Irvine Ranch. Today, hoping to pass on her own philosophy of landscape preservation, Joan Irvine Smith collects and shows the works of California Impressionist painters (1890-1930) at the Irvine Museum. Her belief is that this style of American art can move people to understand the value of saving California's ever rarer landscapes. We hope the same will be true for historic tile and architectural preservation in the state as awareness of our ceramic legacy grows. The former "Pottery Shack" on Highway 101 and the nearby Brayton Laguna Pottery started by Durlin Brayton in 1927 are legends among California ceramic aficionados. Famous for its colorful dinnerware as well as figurines, the earliest Brayton pottery and tiles are now highly coveted by collectors.

The legacy of Newport and Balboa Island as a movie star playground featured strongly here since boating was so much a part of harbor life. Humphrey Bogart and Lauren Bacall kept a boat in Newport Harbor, Jane Russell and Gloria Swanson hung out at the Balboa Bay Club, and Joey Bishop, the last surviving member of the Rat Pack, still lives on Lido Isle, where *Architectural Digest* featured movie stars' homes in a time-honored tradition that continues today with two of actress Diane Keaton's revitalized Spanish Revival homes gracing its covers. And, of course, Orange County's favorite cowboy, John Wayne, called Newport Beach home for 15 years. Wayne's destination of choice was nearby Catalina Island where for many years his arrival drew large crowds of admirers bearing leis on the green Pleasure Pier.

The exterior architecture of this home includes a flat red tile roof and a smooth stucco-finished exterior along with wrought iron trim. The interior finishings evoke European Hotel style with diamond-patterned floor tiles, classic touches in woodworking, and vintage style fixtures set off by dark walnut floors. The kitchen and open living areas have a modern and informal feel, while the clean look of the stainless appliances mixes well with white glass fronted cabinets.

All of these elements provide the backdrop for a world-class California Revival collection of vintage tile murals, romantic Spanish motif paintings, early California plein air paintings, Catalina Island Pottery, and Monterey furniture. Built-in cabinetry and lighting throughout the living areas helps to showcase a rare vintage Bauer pottery collection and an equally museum worthy gathering of rare and colorful Catalina Island Pottery. These collections mix beautifully with contemporary velvet and leather seating, elegant golden touches on gilt accessories, and a mild Asian influence. An eclectic blend of Louis XIVth candelabras and Foo Dogs co-exist happily with vintage Gladding McBean and Catalina oil jars in ironwork and are a perfect expression of the owner's luxurious personal style. The creamy white walls provide a blank canvas for the color explosion that's one of the hallmarks of California Revival decor, while contemporary black and white art photography and sterling silver accessories highlight its versatility. In a state that has always attracted creative types, this home shows that California Revival is a style you can make as unique as your imagination allows, blending modern furnishings with California touches in an individual and eclectic "new classic" style.

Eye-catching Toyon red Catalina Island pottery display on original black and yellow tile checkerboard table with iron base opens onto entry hall.

Simple architecture and the use of fine quality materials in a timeless style evoke an old European hotel. Hand plastered exterior with variegated earth hue. Red tile roof, copper drainpipes, dark French glass paned doors, hand wrought iron balconies, solid mahogany garage doors.

Iron gate enhances private entry surrounded by flowering vines.

Red mahogany front door with Spanish style wrought iron over glass. View of outside mural, Claycraft parrot with flowers which contains fifty tiles set in custom wrought iron frame. Claycraft Tile c1921-39.

Detail of Monterey buffet's crackle and floral painted drawers. Notice cross-hatching style used on leaves.

Painted Monterey buffet in entry set off by light walls and dark wood flooring. Pair of electrified Louis XVI candelabra with warm gold shades. Chinese yellow Bauer Pottery lion pot at center on Asian rosewood pot stand. Antique foo dogs in front of contemporary carved wood mirror. Large vintage palm tree tile in Arts & Crafts frame. Blue Catalina cactus bowl on iron base tile table. Near door a Bauer umbrella stand in yellow with American Encaustic baby Bacchus tile-one of set.

Detail of tile bench by D. & M. Tile Company, Los Angeles, California, 1928-39.

Rare Gladding McBean column pedestal and bowl with boy and dolphin fountain piece in signature mottled turquoise glaze. Boy riding turtle fountain piece sits on iron-based tile table. Hispano Moresque tile bench in original iron and Duncan Gleason (1881-1959) galleon oil painting on wall. Bauer artist Fred Johnson hand thrown garden vases in turquoise and yellow. American Encaustic baby Bacchus tile framed, on entry wall.

Huge Gladding Mc Bean floor vase is a twin to an entrance pot, this time in a vintage dragonhead forged iron stand. Three vintage Catalina Island bird murals in wrought iron frames alongside tall windows; single red parrot, single green parrot, and double red parrots. Large Spanish dancers painting on wall above handrail.

Large period oil painting with softness of lovely Spanish dancers at a fiesta set in a Spanish locale, by period California artist Oscar Knudeson.

Scarce Malibu tile mirror with factory-cast aluminum frame. Large Catalina Island Toyon cactus bowl with mini-cacti and Toyon red display of 14" platter, three scout lamps, and monk book-ends. All on D. & M. tile entry height table with iron base.

Taylor Tilery tropical bird table measures 24". The surround innovatively created with an old steel tire rim. Round tile sets are harder to find and desirable. Catalina and Batchelder field tile border, Malibu pillow tiles on outside edge with a detachable wrought iron base. Eames-era dark brown leather and chrome Wassily chair.

Contemporary living room space with Bauer, Catalina, and San Jose Workshop pottery and tile collection. Period painting of Mexican man on mantel with framed black & white photography and Bauer vases. Fireplace surround black Carrera marble. Clean lines on sofa and club chairs in light color fabrics sit on antique Japanese mat. Old Chinese wood bench, has tight basket woven panel top, used here as coffee table.

Jean-Michelle Frank 1930s design club chairs with one of a pair of unusual, large D. & M. tile tables with heavy iron bases. Catalina Island rope lamp in Descanso green with modern white linen shade. Green step pot by Bauer pottery, Catalina star tile and iron bookends.

Oil painting of a Mexican man smoking on a step, California artist by R. D. Miller, 1902. Two early Bauer Matt Carlton vases appropriately named *California*, one dark green one white. Black and white photography by Brett Weston and Steven Francis.

Glass fronted cabinetry fills either side of fireplace with built-in lighting ideal for collection displays. Pottery by Bauer, Matt Carlton, LAMOSA, Barbara Willis, San Jose Workshop, Garden City, Catalina Island, and Gladding Mc Bean. Plein aire oil painting by Marion Kavanaugh Wachtel (1870-1954).

Detail of the right side of the cabinet, displaying pottery by Bauer, Matt Carlton, Catalina Island, and San Jose Workshop. The glaze colors of these makers mix and match very well.

Catalina Island pottery grouping in blue, yellow, and ivory, compliments tall Bauer stock vase and impressive tile and iron table. Lamps are 19th century French alabaster. Catalina Moorish four tile set in original wood table at left, Malibu round tile table with iron base on right. Gold silk taffeta draperies with white sheers.

Close-up of Tudor Potteries twenty-four tile set on rare long console table with elaborate iron base, c1928.

Corner of dining room with Catalina Island and Taylor Tile table display. Family heirloom sterling tea set on Taylor star patterned round tile set at center. Painting in oil of Victorian home in an orange grove, by contemporary local artist William Dorsey.

Smokey Maple finish Monterey cellaret with iron handles on sides, long hinges, pulls and latch. Three Bauer baby oil jars and San Jose Workshop eight tile pictorial of a man and his pots, in hand-wrought iron frame that incorporates plant holder. Catalina Descanso green ringed pot with cactus.

Powder room with clean, white wood wainscoting, nickel finish on hardware and sink, free standing wash stand in Carrera marble top. Malibu floral pattern tile table with iron galleon design on sides of iron base. Rare pair of 10" hand thrown Bauer oil jars in Chinese yellow and tiny black Rebekah jar attributed to Matt Carlton. Bauer black Indian pot 5" across. Catalina star tile table with iron Deco base. Framed black and white photography and period oil painting of beautiful señorita in flowing red flamenco dress on walls.

Branded Monterey prohibition bar with "Juan Intenoche" style painting on flip-up lid. This bar shows a whimsical rider in oversized sombrero on a wild red horse and cock fighting roosters on the mock "dresser" doors. Catalina orange and black field tile on top with copper covered swing-out sides. Catalina Island Toyon oil jars in matching wrought iron stands on either side. Oil painting of Hispanic man in shadow by California artist R.D. Miller, c1903. Multi-colored cuenca plates by Malibu and Santa Monica Brick Company. On bar, Catalina Toyon scout lamp and wine cups, Moorish plate in orange and black, green cactus flasks, San Jose Workshop painted plate with Mexican dancers, and vintage sterling silver fighting cocks.

Above:
Close-up of Bauer ringware cookie jars from left in Chinese yellow, Delft blue, orange, white, chartreuse, and cobalt. Catalina Island gourd condiment set with tray. Bauer ringware sugar shakers in cobalt and orange. Repeating similar forms in different colors always makes for an appealing display.

Left:
Stainless steel Viking stove provides niche for 16" Bauer oil jars at top in orange and cobalt, a row of ringware cookie jars on shelf, and San Jose Workshop tray on stovetop. On left are a Matt Carlton hand thrown pinch pitcher and a tray in orange, with Bauer baby mugs.

Above:
Festive table set with Catalina Island table settings, candlesticks and pitcher in mixed colors on vintage Mexicana tablecloth. Carved wood Mexican tourist-ware bookends and box. Mexican-style Monterey floral painted chairs with rush seats provide casual seating.

Top left:
Color explosion in cabinet filled with Bauer ringed dinnerware, coffee and tea pots, water jug, and honey pots with Catalina Deco coffee server in yellow and green with demitasse cups. Bauer lion pot, ringed pots and 17" platters top cabinet.

Left:
Detail of Catalina Island table setting showing blue dinner plate, Toyon salad plate, and glass-lined Catalina shrimper in seafoam glaze. Descanso green mug next to Bakelite flatware and small Mexicana box.

Opposite page top:
Spacious kitchen with white cabinets, glass pane doors, stainless steel appliances, and abundant counter space make this an excellent showplace. Catalina Island yellow punch bowl in foreground with two San Jose Workshop sea life themed chargers on left. A multitude of forms and colors of Bauer ringware, oil jars, Matt Carlton vases, as well as Garden City florist vases top kitchen cabinetry. Monterey, rush seat, painted chairs at island.

A wrought iron framed mural of Spanish woman serenading a Spanish man, c1920-30s, California, maker unknown, improves the view outside the kitchen window.

Big, bright yellow Catalina Island punch bowl and multi colored punch cups with great, old, twisted, wrought iron stand. Monterey florals on chair backs show at kitchen table.

Detail of hand painted Mexican folk art style wood kitchen chairs with rush seats by Mason Manufacturing from their Monterey line.

Heirloom sterling teapot on stand, c1800s, large Bauer ringware 14" low salad bowls in Delph blue and orange, with four Catalina Island wood handled coffee servers on period tile trivets in blue, Descanso green, yellow, and Toyon red.

Drawer full of Bakelite flatware and Bakelite bird napkin rings in multiple colors that compliment vintage California pottery.

Jadeite green glass pepper and saltshakers with Mexicana painted wood napkin holder.

Fabulous Catalina Island early monk bookends in bright yellow hold cookbooks next to Bauer artist Matt Carlton's orange pinch pitcher on orange tray holding Bauer "baby" mugs.

Bauer ringed spice jars in three sizes, in black, Chinese yellow, orange, and burgundy, with 17" orange and cobalt platters standing in background on Carrera marble counter and backsplash.

Great Room adjoins kitchen with built in big screen TV. Side cabinets for storage also provide great display space for these larger Bauer, Catalina, and San Jose Workshop collectibles. Contemporary sand colored L-shaped sofa with iron base and an octagonal Hispano Moresque tile coffee table. Monterey side chair with painting, floor lamp with original Mexicana shade. Simple woven window shades in natural straw.

Right:
Display of large Matt Carlton Rebekah jars in Chinese yellow, Delft blue, cobalt blue, and orange, and cobalt Indian pot show well with unusual San Jose Workshop twelve-tile landscape mural of mountain with snow, trees, and water in simple hammered iron frame.

Far right:
San Jose Workshop twelve-tile mural of young Mexican boy with donkey followed by his little black and white dog. Catalina raised design cactus lamp in turquoise with white linen shade and 15" two handled urn. Bauer chartreuse oil jar, ringed pot and stock vase.

Bauer pots and cacti sit on vintage tile tables looking out upon relaxing harbor view. Monterey floor lamp with original shade has tile base. Bronze silk taffeta draperies and white sheers cover large picture windows.

Monterey bar in a custom two-toned finish with orange painted hardware, and a signed "Juan Intenoche" painting of a Mexican charro or bull rider. Garden City yellow oil jars on iron stands. Monterey daybed in old red finish with vintage pillows, and Mexican saltillo. Romantic Spanish couple painting by A. Ruelle, Mexico, c1930-40s, and period Western desert painting.

Monterey buffet topped with D. & M. tile inserts in old wood finish. Pair of Descanso green Catalina Island trophy lamps with goat hide shades, 19th century English Chinoiserie box with collection of vintage California tourist mission bells on top. 19th century Mexican, carved wood Santos is reflected in period iron and tile mirror.

A tile mural from one of the San Jose Workshops of Señor and Señorita courting under street lamp, over master jetted tub with contemporary wrought iron frame. Garden City early oil jar in turquoise, GMB soap dishes, and Bauer turquoise bowl on iron stand.

Taylor Tilery Spanish style dancer triptych framed in custom ironwork, from left: a two-tile lady, a six- tile couple, and a two-tile man. Small Italian vanity and mirror from 18th century, with original hand painting of climbing pink roses on Spanish green background. Same dancing couple tile is shown in original wood table to right. Period china señorita figurine, European maker. Chinoiserie box is 18th century tea caddy.

White on white bathroom uses distinctive 1" octagon black and white mosaic tiles and accepts any decor. Monterey pot stand with handle holds Bauer Spanish pots in black and chartreuse glaze. Bauer jade green oil jar and Indian pot. Desert mural by D. & M. tile in simple hand hammered iron frame. Mexicana folk art crackle painting with tacked leather corners by "Eduardo."

Master bedroom features eye-catching wrought iron, heart scroll headboard. Neutral bedding and woven shades keep serenity the focus with colorful pottery and tile as accents. Large Catalina Island blue, two-handled, urn lamp on Japanese tansu to right, shorter Catalina seafoam lamp on Taylor dragon tile desk to left, have white linen shades. Tall Staffordshire spaniels on either side of bed in gold and white, Chinoiserie pattern on yellow background throw pillow.

Ornate wrought iron table base supports this square tile set with an integrated floral design and matching borders by Gladding McBean. Staffordshire 6" poodles, c1800s. Catalina Island Toyon lamp base with stitched parchment shade.

Sitting area in master bedroom with D. & M. heraldic tiles in hammered iron fire screen. Largest Bauer #100 oil jars in cobalt and Chinese yellow on either side. To left sits Gladding McBean floral table pictured prior. Taylor Tilery tropical bird tile table foreground. M antel displays Catalina Island mini oil jars in an array of glazes. Large D. & M. knight tile at center of triptych display with matching handmade iron frames. Butter yellow suede sofa and armchair by Roche Bobois and Chippendale side chair in right corner. Right wall vintage Catalina Island crane tile set in oak wood frame .

Mantel displays fine collection of Catalina Island mini oil jars from left in caramel brown, two multicolored experimental glaze jars, Toyon red, black, teal green, Descanso green, blue, and turquoise. D. & M. 12" knight tile in full regalia, two side tiles are shields in the same color palette with matching contemporary hand-made iron frames.

Hillside Pottery garden jar with signature band of tile and shards around center stands 32" tall and smaller Hillside style partner nestled in corner of garden.

Left:
Patio setting with two Catalina Island, six-sided backgammon tile planters, c1930s, and tall vintage Hillside Pottery concrete and tile urn.

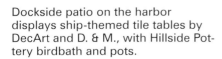

Dockside patio on the harbor displays ship-themed tile tables by DecArt and D. & M., with Hillside Pottery birdbath and pots.

CALIFORNIA REVIVAL:

DECORATIVE ARTS: 1920S TO 1940S

Art Tile and Pottery, Paintings, Photography, Furniture, Folk Art, Textiles, and Metalwork

The vast scope and diversity of vintage Golden Era decorative arts created during the 1930s Spanish Revival movement can be intimidating even for an experienced designer, let alone a new collector. The main problem is where to start and the questions are usually the same: "Is it real or repro?," "How do I know it's what (or made by whom) they say it is?," or the hard-to-answer "What is available?" With images ordered here by theme, and not simply by maker, one can begin to *see* the answer to these questions.

Pottery: In the 1930s scores of California art pottery companies flourished. They used artisans and craftsmen to design their vases, lamps, candlesticks, bookends, novelties, and other forms both by hand and by molding techniques. Top ceramists' known as "color men" were hired to develop distinctive glazes, and mold makers hand carved original designs for execution in clay. Listed California artists painted plaques and created mural designs. All were made with aesthetics in mind, but had a strong utilitarian streak. Many companies also had a sideline in colorful patio ware and tablewares known as industrial artwares. A few companies made both tiles *and* pottery, notably Catalina Clay Products Company, maker of Catalina Island Pottery and Tile, Brayton Laguna of Laguna Beach, and Gladding, McBean and Company of Glendale and Lincoln, California.

Tile: Period California tile was made by over a hundred companies in the state during the Golden Era prior to World War II. Recurring themes such as ships, birds, geometrics, and florals, found in forms such as tables, single tiles, or murals, make for lots of choices. Some collections focus on maker according to the locale where they were based, like Malibu, Avalon, Santa Monica, or Berkeley. Enjoyable color combinations are another way to refine your display, with glazes and techniques either subtle or bold. Vintage tiles from San Antonio, Texas, made by any of the San Jose Workshops (see *Terminology*) are also included in California Revival homes for many reasons, their artistic quality, colorful glazes, and Mexicana themes among them.

Themes and forms: Some people have special themes in a room or wall of their home, while others maintain the same look throughout the entire house. Others

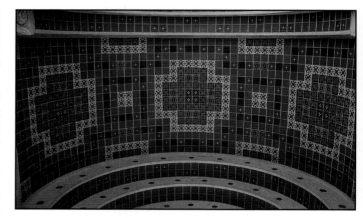

Catalina tile archway at the Wrigley Botanical Gardens in Avalon on Catalina Island. (*Photo courtesy of Carole Coates.*)

prefer to mix vintage touches with modern elements for a truly individual style. You might find your Arts and Crafts bungalow looks great with a "Monterey" bedroom, or, if you live near the water, decide to use oceanic imagery in tile, or, if in a scenic country setting, choose California-themed oil paintings of people for balance. Individuality is key. Favorite colors, patterns, and forms are a good place to begin. If you like photography or advertising art, postcards or prints, fabrics or metalwork, important modern paintings or unknown local artists, they can all be seen through the lens of California Revival. Starting with a few trial pieces is one way to make sure you're going in the right direction for your home, but you might already know what you like and prefer to start big. A novice collector in the Wine Country studied Bauer Pottery books and surprised a local dealer by beginning her collection with a combination of large Bauer, Pacific, and Garden City oil jars for her front door. Ten years later they are still favorite pieces. A good reference library will help you find additional examples from vintage makers and enable you to make more informed buying decisions. (See *Bibliography*.)

Preservation: Think about mounting vintage scenic tiles in wood or in iron framing so they can be used inside or out (preferably on a sturdy wall, protected from the elements), then if you sell your home, you can take your vintage tile treasures with you to make sure they are preserved. Vintage tiles can be expertly framed with a "window" cutout to show clay and/or any important markings. Remember to get expert help hanging heavy murals so they are secure. Check out less expensive California-made reproduction tiles if your budget doesn't allow buying vintage, or always use reproduction tiles if your intention is to permanently install them in walls and on floors. Try to see the tiles in person or order samples to make sure colors and quality suit you. (Visit the book's web site at www.californiarevival.com for resources and recommendations.)

Ships & Oceanic Themes

Spanish galleons with banners flying, lithe sailboats, ocean liners, and harbor scenes enliven many of the California Revival decorative arts. Leaping marlins, undersea garden scenes, and pottery shells, ranging from the realistic to the fantastic enliven living room walls, patios, and bedrooms, and are found on plates, tables, paintings, and textiles.

High shelf filled with Catalina Island Pottery coffee servers, mugs, and gourd shaped salt and peppers in a variety of colorful glazes. Seahorse plate with cobalt borders comes from *Undersea Garden* series by Catalina, early 1930s. Framed *Catalina is Calling Me* sheet music is early 1900s. Santa Catalina poster advertisement by American graphic artist, Otis Shepard. Stunning twenty-tile Viking ship and gulls mural by Gladding McBean in original thin wooden frame.

Commissioned, contemporary tile mural depicting Richard Henry Dana's ship, *Pilgrim* inset over fireplace. Catalina Island Pottery conch shell vases in Toyon red and white flank one in blue by Van Briggle, shown on mantel made of cast concrete with stone finish and clamshell detail.

Spanish galleon at sea on 6" tiles attributed to Taylor Tilery, California, c1930. Originally mounted in simple wood table that broke down over time, tiles were salvaged and set in iron framework by artisans specially trained in removal, restoration, and setting of historic tile murals.

Gladding McBean *Galleon Taking Sail* mural with 2" border tiles and contemporary hand hammered iron frame.

Malibu Pottery mural of Spanish galleon on rough seas, consisting of twenty tiles. Ornate contemporary iron frame with shield and ship flags.

Malibu Potteries *Modern Liner* single tile measures twelve by twelve inches and is one in a series of historic vessels created by the company during the 1920s.

Gladding McBean mural entitled *Sailing to Catalina* is glazed in a three-color graphic style and is based on magazine cover art by Lewis Carleton Ryan, c1932, in original wooden framing.

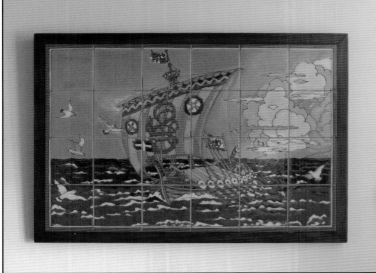

Gladding McBean *Viking Ship at Full Sail* twenty-four tile mural is a dramatic depiction of action on choppy seas in original wooden framing.

Trio of vintage Catalina Island plates. Top down: Catalina Women's Golf Tournament "trophy" plate, hand painted and personalized, given to top players in the 1930s, Seagull hand painted plate by Catalina artist Frances Graham, and Spanish galleon design glazed by hand in six different colors before firing. Notice difference between "cold painted" plates executed on top of pre-glazed plates with actual paint, and decorative plates that were hand glazed and then fired to achieve their final form (see *Terminology* section for more information).

Catalina Island pottery and tile in Descanso green set off by the elegant white mantel and walls. California artist Joe Duncan Gleason, also famous as an author (see *Bibliography*), book illustrator, and maritime expert, executed this oil painting of a historic sailing vessel at sea, c1930s.

Impressive large Catalina Island punchbowl, and graphic "tea tile" trivets, both in Monterey brown glaze. Shown here on Eames-era chrome, glass, and travertine table with caramel colored leather and chrome *Cantilever* chairs by Mart Stam, c1926.

Dramatic sailboats at harbor feature in this oil by Santa Barbara artist Fredrick A. Pawla (1876-1964). Off white walls and soft lighting create a gallery feel in hallway. Taylor Tilery console table on ornate iron anchors the space and Catalina blue bulbous vase in iron holder echoes the ocean colors.

Catalina Island *Kissing Fish* tile in Descanso green glaze is 6" square in solid oak Arts and Crafts frame. So called "tea tiles" could stand alone as a trivet since the sides were glazed all around.

Completely unique and now-historic bird and fish murals made by Catalina Island Pottery in the early 1930s are as vibrant and appealing as they were the day they were made. *Leaping Marlin* mural in iron framework, four 6" tiles make the scene with Toyon red borders and cobalt corners.

Stylized sea creature blows bubbles in a pale pink sea, done in heavy cuenca style in this four-tile set produced by the Solon and Schemmel (S & S) Tile Company, San Jose, California, c1930s, set in dark oak Arts & Crafts frame.

Colorful sea theme created on mantel with pieces created by Catalina Island Pottery c1927-1937. Swordfish platter centerpiece is executed in raised design and glazed in Descanso green. On left: high gloss yellow and Toyon red nautilus shell vases (made later in different glazes by Gladding McBean, c1940s). On right: green starfish ashtray, red conch shell, and large green clamshell.

Eye catching display of plaques from the *Undersea Garden* series by Catalina Island Pottery, all with deep cobalt blue borders. From left: seahorse, shark, and undersea garden in two sizes.

More color possibilities in Catalina Island Pottery's *Undersea Garden* theme plates. From left Toyon red seahorse, blue sea garden, yellow seahorse, turquoise sea garden, red sea garden plate, and yellow ringed flower pot, all c1929-1935.

Fantasy mermaid tile niche designed by contemporary artists (see book's web site for *Resources*), known for their work in private homes as well as on Catalina Island. In recent years they executed the late set designer John Gabriel Beckman's famous Casino mermaid design in tile, as well as many other tile commissions on the Island. Step down bath and overhead shower are encased in two shades of green, reproduction Catalina tile sets flank the steps, and hexagonal floor tiles make for a non-slip floor.

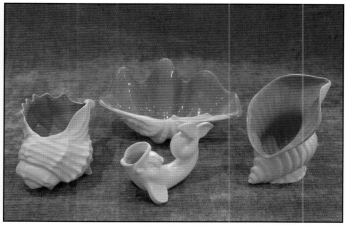

Gladding, McBean & Co. pottery sign, contemporary, 2005. Gladding (often called simply *GMB*) has been in continuous business in Lincoln, California, since the turn of the 19th century. They were one of very few pottery and tile companies to survive the depression and did so by acquiring the competition, as well as by making sewer pipe. They bought the name *Catalina* in 1937 and used some of their molds up to the early 1940s with different glazes and markings. Collectors use this shorthand: if it says "*Catalina Pottery*" (instead of "Catalina Island Pottery," or "Catalina," or "Catalina Island") or has an ink stamp "Make in U.S.A." it was made in Los Angeles by Gladding, McBean & Co., so "*Pottery*" means it's L.A. or mainland pottery, and "Island" means it's Island-made. (Check *Bibliography* for further study.)

Seashells and stylized dolphin in GMB's highly recognizable style. The dolphin is also found in solid pastel colors, late 1930s.

Historic Catalina Island children's bowl and cup set has an artist's rendition of children and their toys on the beach at Avalon with the Casino in the background. A Catalina artist (most likely Francis Graham) created this set as a customized baby gift in the early 1930s. Sometimes given to employees' children or very special (and we hope careful) little ones.

Examples of Gladding McBean pottery shell-shaped vases. Some used Catalina molds from the Island days, some were slightly redesigned from the late 1930s. Catalina Island pioneered the use of two-tone glazing in their later years and Gladding continued the trend. These three seashell vases have matte white exteriors and glossy pastel colored interiors.

Historic Catalina Island Pottery children's cup and bowl set showing custom signatures on bottom. "Santa Catalina Island" hand painted on bottom of cup, by artist in cold paint.

Stack of Gladding McBean two color, shell-shaped serving dishes, white exterior, turquoise and peach pastel interior. Often Gladding pieces are ink stamped "Catalina Pottery Made in U.S.A."

Spanish, Hispanic, and Mexican Influences

Craftsmen, artists, designers, and other hardworking men and women of Mexican heritage contributed enormously to the Spanish Revival movement of the 1930s. A large and diverse Hispanic population lived and worked in and around Los Angeles, where many of the important creative companies of the period were based. Group pictures at Mason Manufacturing's Monterey plant, and Catalina Island Pottery, taken in 1937 show many employees of Latino extraction. A Mexican artist/cartoonist/animator was the head of Monterey's famed painting department. Some Mexican families came to the United States during the early 1900s to flee the Mexican Revolution; many have lived in Southern California for generations as descendants of *Californios* when California *was* Mexico, and many had useful skills and trades that were highly valued. As a thematic element both Mexican and romanticized Spanish figures were hugely popular and Hispanic artists did much of the work, although Mexico's German and European residents and visitors/artists were captivated by the subject matter as well. Today, vintage Mexican and early Californian folk art, fine oil paintings, watercolors, murals, photography, tile, pottery, wooden plaques, metalwork, wrought iron, ad-

vertising pieces, tourist wares, and other historic work that depicts Mexican scenes and people are highly sought after by California and Californiana collectors of all ethnic backgrounds, not because they contain occasional stereotypes, but because it is a reflection of the sometimes distorted way things *were* seen and a way of acknowledging the difference. Some collectors focus on the more egregious Mexican stereotypical art as a political statement (see following essay). Ethel Wilson Harris, who founded and ran many of the San Jose workshops in San Antonio, Texas, made frequent trips to Mexico for research, inspiration, and to find employees and artists to create original designs for their tile murals, taking great care to get the details right. Whether a whimsical depiction of a señor riding a burro on a wooden plaque, a romanticized Aztec warrior on calendar art, or a WPA era mural recognized as a masterpiece, the art and craft tradition of Mexico continues to be an important component of California style today that has long been undervalued and unappreciated. California Revival enthusiastically recognizes and embraces California's Mexican art and craft heritage and roots along with Spanish, Native American, and rancho traditions.

One of several "trademarks," "signatures," or "logos," sometimes found on tile and pottery created by the productive San Jose Workshops, San Antonio, Texas, 1929 to 1977. This mark represents a *maguey* agave (also known as a Century Plant) in full bloom and is the characteristic craftsman mark of Ethel Wilson Harris who oversaw the creative output of many of the workshops (see *Terminology* for a list of the workshops). Not all of this vintage pottery and tile is marked and one must be savvy about recent reproductions.

Collecting Mexicana:
Redefining Stereotypes

Jose R. Padilla & Deborah Escobedo,
Youth and Farmworker Rights Attorneys,
San Francisco, California

We are public interest lawyers who have spent our entire legal careers representing the Latino/Mexican immigrant communities of California. We began to collect Mexican and Latino folk and fine art primarily for cultural reasons, but also as part of our personal "politic." On the one hand, our collection reflects our families' working class roots (one from rural California, the other from Los Angeles). It is common art from the hands and minds of common folk, like the communities that raised us. Ironically, as part of our larger collection, we have come to collect a type of folk art that others might find offensive, yet we find affirming because we have redefined it as a personal art form that strangely fits our working lives.

Some years ago, we attended a fundraiser at the home of an African-American judge, and were startled to find the house full of what appeared to be racist icons, Aunt Jemima, Little Black Sambo, pickaninny art. Upon asking "why," the judge indicated that the art was a historical reminder of how a dominant society will have negative, ethnic stereotype in its art forms, as a reflection of the social condition of the ethnic group and to diminish the social character of that community. His collection was an affirmative reminder of how far his community had come, but at the same time served as a symbolic incentive regarding the distance left to go. The negative caricaturing of ethnic communities is as old as the country and it appears that no group has escaped this scorn. But for some groups, the art is persistent and deeper only because the integration of these communities into the social fabric is still a work in progress. Ironically, the mind set that wants all Americans to be the same, will still persist in caricaturing difference in an almost mindless yet creative manner.

As collectors, this same notion is found in the skewed image of the "Sleeping-Mexican" icon that we have collected in so many diverse forms. It is a symbol that takes on even greater meaning today, given how Mexican immigration has consumed the national dialogue. But for us, it is an affirmation of change that is in process and that we choose to celebrate through this icon, in all its multitude of forms that skilled artisans, many of them Mexicans, have so creatively transformed: leaning against cacti, palm trees, liquor barrels, made in wood, ceramic, plaster, tin; as lamps, bookends, thermometers, golf caps, salt-pepper shakers, matchbooks, crackle plaques, napkin holders and as Mexican silver pins. For us, the only "standards" we have are that the folk art piece be vintage; characterized by the "sleeping or resting" posture; and that it be faceless. In most forms we have, the image is "touristy," promoted, generally, as cheap (affordable) Mexican tourist souvenir. In our home the collection is displayed with two vintage books entitled *Mañana Land* and *Wetback*.

As public interest lawyers, this art gives us a cultural visual of how a community can, artistically, be given a false stereotypical image, caricatured in a manner quite opposite of what we have found in representing the interests of its people. This working immigrant and citizen community values family responsibility; values religious belief; values hard work and the notion that you earn what you have. Because this is a community to which we have given our legal careers, we appreciate this unique art form that we have re-defined to be iconic, not of how things are, but of a social error that we strive to correct in all of its disaffirming forms.

Lively Mexican village mural utilizes many of the San Jose Workshop characters and settings. Unusual creamy white background with a folk art feel in a large twenty-four tile format. The WPA-era studios run by Ms. Harris actively recruited Mexican artisans to work in Texas to produce authentic scenes and Mexican themed designs; custom contemporary wrought iron frame based on authentic period style.

One of the San Jose Workshops created this mural entitled *La Paloma*, with a guitarist serenading his lady *La Tehuana* who wears the traditional dress from Tehuantepec in the state of Oaxaca, dove in hand. Fifteen 6" tiles make the scene, with borders, set in a contemporary iron frame with a growing plant motif modeled on vintage ironwork.

San Jose Workshop tile scene entitled *Huapango* shows a couple dancing the Mexican folk dance from Veracruz of the same name. The epitome of craftsmanship in tile style, this scene has a painterly design and shows people and activities along with of a real sense of life and movement. Original wrought iron table base holds eight 8" tiles. A version of this scene is installed in a wall at the historic San Jose Mission home of Ethel Wilson Harris (1893-1984) in San Antonio, Texas.

Two colorful San Jose Workshop tile tables. On the left, a Señorita dances while a guitar player sings, visually framed under the archway of a grand hacienda. A multicolored array of tiles borders the scene. On the right, Mexican dancers 8" single tile center with green and orange borders. Both tables in original vintage iron bases.

San Jose Workshops mural entitled *Xochimilco*. This fifteen-tile scene depicts a man piloting his boatload of flowers with his lovely lady passenger. A famous water canal retreat on the outskirts of Mexico City referred to as Mexico's "Venice," it's still used today for market gardens in Mexico City.

Two San Jose Workshop scenic tables with vintage wrought iron bases. From top, Mexican man rides his donkey home from market, baskets empty, his wife carries pots on her back. Bottom table shows beautiful señorita dancing in classic costume while playing castanets on a grand veranda. Notice tile flooring that creates a "tile on tile" effect.

One of the San Jose Workshops made this lively scenic tile table showing a restaurant theme, a "Rosetta stone" in tile, it features many of the characters found in other tile scenes. (*Photo courtesy of Robert Benson.*)

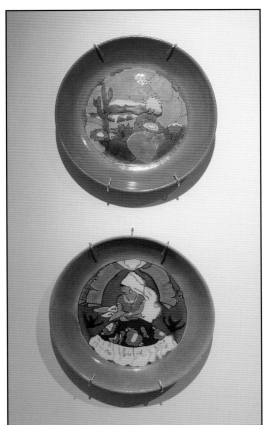

San Jose Workshop wall plaques in large 14" bowl form make an impression. Top is hacienda scene with orange glazed border, bottom is a medium view of *La Tehuana* (see prior captions) with lilies and bluebirds in detail, green glazed border.

San Jose Workshops colorful scenic plates, in unusual red clay and 9" size, depict many domestic scenes and characters that can be found in tile form as well. Attributed to the Mexican Arts and Crafts workshop (1929 to 1939), which is one of the makers defined as being in the San Jose Workshops movement (see *Terminology*).

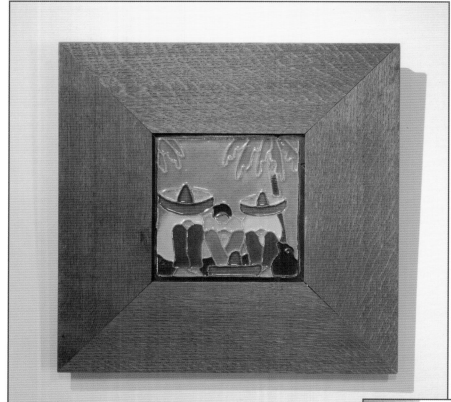

Colorful single pictorial tile of three amigos by Brayton Laguna Pottery. Dark Mission wooden frame allows wall display. (See *Decorative Arts* chapter for more Brayton.)

Catalina Island made Descanso green hexagon tile set in Island-made wooden base is a hard to find bedside table height. On top, Catalina's *Siesta Man* pipe holder, ashtray and match holder combination in matte blue glaze and cold painted details. Vintage matchbook design by graphic artist Otis Shepard. Smoking accessories figured prominently in Catalina's line and are very popular with collectors. Monterey green crackle painted wood and iron detail hurricane lamp, hand painted finish and flowers.

Bauer Pottery vases were often bisque fired but not glazed and then cold painted by enterprising Mexican artists who embellished them with Mexicana themes in Los Angeles for the tourist trade. Three pots on right are Bauer, pot on left is of Mexican origin but painted by the same artist in Los Angeles during the 1940s.

Rare, large Brayton Laguna Pottery pictorial plaque featuring a Mexican folk art caricature and sporting a cobalt blue border. Brayton Laguna was founded in Laguna Beach in 1920s and was known for their rich glazes in mix-and-match dinnerware. Bauer cobalt blue one pint, one quart, and two quart ringed pitchers and large fruit bowl sit on stainless steel counter. "Ten gallon" hat in cobalt by Bauer, small cobalt sombrero by San Jose Workshop. Massing your display with a range of vintage items in similar glazes creates visual impact.

A pair of romantic *Señor* and *Señorita* tiles by D. & M. Tile, Los Angeles, California, in an unusual size, twelve by four inches; simple contemporary iron holders were created to hang the art and to keep the backs open for identification and study. Right wall, a four-tile portion of a larger San Jose Workshop mural shows Mexican couples at a party while a pigtailed young lady sits out the dance, in custom made iron frame. Large S & S (Solon & Schlemmel) tile entry or console table with subtle muted colored tiles show deep cuenca technique (see *Terminology* section). Bauer Indian pot in orange with bromeliads.

Caballero courting beautiful señorita depicted on this muted tone tile set in an unusual matte finish by Taylor Tilery, c1930-1941; hand twisted contemporary iron frame. One of a series of high quality six-tile murals by Taylor featuring Spanish and Mexican themes that did not use high gloss glazing.

Spanish dancer, six-tile mural in costume, down to the fringe detail on her shawl. Bold color and subtle design make for a nice contrast on this scene by Taylor Tilery, Los Angeles, California, in simple "Catalina style" iron frame.

Tile mural entitled *Spanish Trovador* [sic] from series created by Taylor Tilery using earth tone color palette and same scale. This tile set shows a young suitor singing to his senorita from her courtyard. Hand made twisted iron frame is contemporary.

A Spanish dancer mural with an Art Deco twist. Thick glazing and brilliant colors, castanets, Flamenco guitarist near a cobalt tree, and a built-in "river of life" border make this an outstanding scene. Attributed to Taylor Tilery; present day iron frame.

Spanish guitarist in formal clothing, unusual vertical format utilizes three 6" tiles to make the scene, attributed to Taylor Tilery. Vintage wrought iron frame with plant holder; yellow pot by Catalina Island Pottery.

Mural-sized oil painting of a celebration in the courtyard of a very large hacienda or mission. This painting's oversized nature makes it perfect for a large home or public installation. Notice lack of male dancers, in what might have been a traditional ladies-only dance. This joyous piece portrays movement in pastel tones imparting a soft, tapestry look. By little known artist Oscar Knudeson, early to mid 1900s.

Malibu Potteries tile wall display (from left) 8" tile of lovely senorita, 6" tile of senorita in formal attire, Spanish galleon at sea, handsome Spanish man in formal dress, 8" Spanish Conquistador. Iron frames are period cast and painted aluminum.

Lovely oil painting portrayal of Spanish man and woman flirting in a doorway. The trappings of everyday life are seen in the pottery and flowers but the romance is quintessential Oscar Theodore Jackman (1878-1940), known as an illustrator whose prints graced the showrooms and catalogs of Barker Brothers and Monterey furniture. Bedroom has pale butter colored walls that show off both oil painting and Monterey headboard with hand detailed florals and vintage camp blanket bedding.

Two period oil paintings by Ralph Davidson Miller (1858-1945) give a Mexicana feel to this Great Room. One is entitled *In a Mexican Patio*, with an original Barker Brothers tag.

An intriguing oil painting of a Spanish man, by California artist R.D. Miller, c1879, casts a moody ambiance. Rich, earthy colors, and original textured wood and gesso frame contrast with white walls. Understated Descanso green Catalina urns, tile, and candle lamp with iron.

Period oil painting of a beautiful Spanish dancer in a bold red and black color scheme, executed in a graphic style. In traditional costume, the señoritas silk embroidered and fringed shawl floats across the canvas. Fine example of Spanish Revival art, initialed by unknown artist, dated 1930.

This "scandalous" oil painting seems to hide an untold mystery worthy of a *CSI* episode. The shaded character smokes, appears reflective, and has a knife stuck into the seat he occupies. A relaxing smoke after a knife fight perhaps? Beautifully executed by well-known female artist Muriel Sibell Wolle (1898-1977) and dedicated "To Crosby," she often painted moody subjects such as miners and other hard working types

Handsome Caballero at the marketplace mural was perhaps a section of a larger wall mural, c1930s-1940s, artist unknown. Large three by five foot section on board executed in a graphic art style. Many murals were done in this period in public places inspired by the famed mural work of Diego Rivera and David Alfaro Siqueiros. Luckily this fragment was salvaged and framed. Catalina Island Pottery collection in matte green glaze on Tudor tile-top console table with wrought iron base.

Whimsical Monterey folk art known today as a "Juan Intenoche" painting was one of a large series created by a moonlighting Disney artist of Mexican heritage possibly using a pseudonym. His signature is not legible, perhaps on purpose. George Mason, designer of the Monterey Furniture line, c1929-1945, preferred floral painting, but the cartoon art was wildly popular and eventually the man known as "Juan" became head of the painting department. Painting on board of the Mexican cartoon character with his trademark giant moustache (which might even be a self-caricature of the artist) on an even wilder spotted horse jumping a cactus. (See *Terminology* section or visit www.findingjua-nintonoche.com to learn more.)

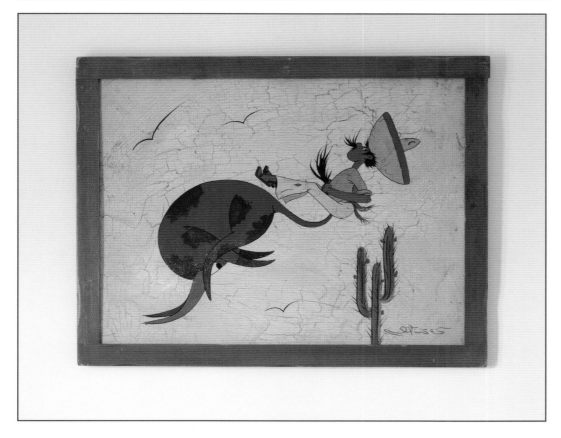

Original Monterey painting with crackle background, Mexicana character, snorting bull, and cactus in original painted wood frame. Quite often, like cartoon frames, these paintings showed a passive restful scene, followed by one of intense action. Some have "before and after" characteristics. Painted on furniture as well as on wood plaques, beware of current day reproduction paintings on lampshades and furniture that are not clearly marked as new.

Another recurring animal character often found in Monterey paintings is the comical donkey. The stubborn donkey with exaggerated features and expressions often seems to frustrate his owner. Crackle painted on board, original painted frame.

Crackle painting on board, attributed to Monterey as a "Juan Intenoche." Barefoot Mexican man walking donkey loaded with apples. Many other Mexican folk artists did crackle-ware paintings with similar themes during this same Spanish Revival period, some signed, others not.

Young Spanish bride and groom painted on board with crackle texture and cacti background by A. Ruelle, Mexico, c1930s-1940s, known for many folk art paintings in this style.

Large period oil painting on canvas, the scene portrayed is of a mother and father from a wealthy Mexican family expressing pride to their young son. Original gesso gilt frame. Painting by H. Graf, c1929.

Large pictorial Spanish Revival iron garden gate painted to match room decor and used as wall hanging.

Sepia tone image by noted photographer, Hugo Brehme, c1920s, famous for his rural and authentic Mexican scenes.

Mexican print advertisement for "Ron Siesta" rum showing the Monterey character in his trademark giant sombrero on spotted red horse, signed. Sunny yellow wall over a Corona beer cooler lends a cantina ambiance.

Vintage Mexican folk art paper mache donkey. George Mason's Monterey Furniture line included accessories like this signed, hand made iron donkey lamp with leather saddle for holding cigarette packs on each side. Hugely popular when sold at Bullocks Wilshire and Barker Brothers. Original hand painted parchment shade.

Monterey side chair in old wood finish, with donkey and Mexican stereotypical folk art garden pieces. These small, well-loved creations are not as typical as the larger ones, and this pair is usually kept indoors. Mexican "siesta" figures are an advertising symbol still in use today in Mexico and the U.S. to designate Mexican places of business, primarily restaurants. (See *Collecting Mexicana: Redefining Stereotypes.*)

Scenic San Jose Workshop mural shows a potter carrying his wares down to a village. These eight beautifully executed tiles combine to achieve an example of the artistic mastery these workshops achieved. Set in a contemporary iron frame and potholder with Catalina Island ringed planter in Descanso green.

Mission, Western, and Landscape

Spain's Franciscan Missionaries came to Alta California in the 1700s and transformed the landscape in their quest to colonize the land. They represented both church and state until their success in creating industry and great wealth (using Native Americans as indentured servants) made their purpose obsolete. Garrisons and towns sprang up along with great jealousy of the church's properties. The settlers won, the Missions were secularized, lands and riches fought over and dispersed, and the Missions and their remaining Native Americans fell mostly to ruin. The Missions were rediscovered and rebuilt in the early 1900s by Californians seeking the region's historic past. The romance of the missions helped to fuel a mission craze in building, art, design, and tourism. This Mission Revival period led to a renewed interest in California's Spanish and Mexican past and sparked the Spanish Colonial movement (with its European roots), followed shortly by the Spanish Revival that additionally drew upon Mexican and Spanish traditions in the New World.

Western influences have long been a staple of American art and crafts and it's only natural that cowboys, cattle, wagon trains, oxen, and ten gallon hats would be a popular design theme "out west" from the 1920s to 1950s in California, Arizona, New Mexico, Nevada, Wyoming, Texas, Colorado, and beyond. California-made, vintage western tiles, paintings, textiles, pottery novelties, and ephemera are probably as popular now as then.

The colors of California have probably inspired more art than any other state in the country. It certainly is the home to some very important art movements and schools such as the California Watercolor Society, plein air artists, Laguna Colony, Carmel Art Association, the Otis Art Institute, and the Chouinard Art Institute to name a few. Museums and private collections are filled with fine examples both representational and impressionistic that attest to the California Style. Landscape scenes in oil, watercolor, and tile, painted on plates, et al are a top decorative element of California Revival whether valued period art or high quality works by contemporary California artists.

Taylor Tilery scenic tile set depicting El Mirador Hotel, Palm Springs, California, c1930-1941. Wood frame surround from original tabletop.

Taylor Tilery courtyard scene with a Spanish gentleman in bullfighter costume and a young señorita. The intricate architectural details add a rich touch. Contemporary wrought iron frame with hand hammered bell.

Left:
A Monterey buffet's festive tile top holds a collection of vintage metal mission bells originally sold to tourists in the early 1920s to 1940s. They are miniature versions of the California bells, which were placed roadside during the early 1900s along the historic mission trail El Camino Real, now Highway 101.

More vintage mission bells. Renewed interest in California's Spanish, Mexican, and Native American history led to the restoration of the then crumbling mission chain in the early 1900s. Tourists flocked to see the newly restored missions and souvenirs of every type became very popular along with interest in everything about old California.

Built-in alcove holds sepia and hand tinted photographs of California missions, c1900s, matted in a soft neutral color, along with a small collection of vintage mini-mission bells. Twenty-one missions from San Diego to Sonoma were built in the 1700s by the Franciscans and their Indian neophytes, and were left to ruin after secularization.

Grouping of scarce Taylor Tilery tables with lone Indian on the plains, c1930s. Note the covered wagons down in the valley (echoed in other Taylor scenes) and the different glazing styles and colorations. Pair of round floral tile tables in iron bases by D. & M. Tile, Los Angeles, California, 1928-1939.

Old signs and graphics from the period can add depth and just plain fun. Ranch entry sign in hammered copper reads "Tres Campañas," translated as "Three Bells," perhaps a play on words or an architectural feature.

Contemporary great room painted creamy white sets off Bauer and Catalina pottery on mantel and on room divider. Lone Indian scenic by Taylor Tilery, framed in custom iron with arrowhead detail. Pair of wrought iron floor candelabra, c1920-1939s. Descanso green pottery display on mantel by Catalina Island.

Scarce tile table desert scene attributed to Tudor Potteries, Los Angeles. Tudor is known for this blurry, yet painterly technique.

Catalina Island display includes cactus bowl in smaller of two sizes in Toyon red filled with pottery cactus shakers in assorted glazes, deco water jug and mini oil jar in Toyon red.

Cactus and Mexicana whimsies made of copper, pot metal, iron and wood make a fun grouping, c1930s-1940s.

Detail showing Catalina Island white, ringed planter and cacti in original iron ivy-design holder, with two matte green, raised design cactus flask candleholders.

Vintage orchid cactus oil painting, unsigned, in green and red hues shown over redwood mantel with terracotta tile fireplace surround topped with vintage Malibu border tiles. Mantel shown in various ways to illustrate how details can be changed when the look needs refreshing, or to accommodate a new acquisition. Catalina Island Pottery in Descanso green continues the red and green complimentary color scheme. Pair of period hand wrought iron floor candelabra, with colorful Bauer oil jars above.

Hand tinted photo of cacti in bloom in original gilt frame, c1920s.

Taylor Tilery cacti and covered wagon, two tile sets designed as a pair, framed in iron. Vintage California revival style colored draperies.

Mixing it up with western-themed tiles and art pottery from diverse makers. D. & M. tile oxen and wagons in iron frames, San Jose Workshops' single sheriff tile in original frame and cowboy on horse plate, and Catalina Island painted plate shows a cowboy on a wild stallion. Bauer collection shows behind glass doors of kitchen cabinetry.

Custom designs of hand wrought iron frames add to beauty of single tile murals by San Jose Workshops and D. & M. Tile.

From one of the San Jose Workshops: heavy clay bookends came in two sizes and were hand glazed in four or five of their most popular designs.

Catalina Island Pottery created this simple child's set of cup, bowl and plates, which unwittingly became a historic museum piece when it was hand painted in 1934 by one of Catalina's artists for William Wrigley, Jr. His nickname "Billy" is painted on rim of cereal bowl along with a horse and rider.

Underside of hand painted child's set with signature written in paint under glaze, and around the impressed Catalina Island factory mark: *Billy from Daddy and Momma on Easter 1934.*

Rarely seen hand-tooled leather top, with cacti, long horn steer heads, and rope pattern edge decorates this side table made by Mason's Monterey Furniture. Often pieces were painted or custom designed to order. Their western-themed designs work well in cabins, lodges, or ranch homes, either period or contemporary.

An arched window filled with sunlight is ideal for display of Catalina Island Pottery cowboy hat collection. In a rainbow of colorful glazes, the cowboy hats complete the Catalina Room concept, which the owners devised for their collection. Small felt Spanish Gaucho hat with pompoms at center was a souvenir for Catalina Island tourists of the 1930s.

Mexican sombreros are featured in the stairway landing of this Spanish Revival home located in Long Beach, California. Hats were added to wooden French wine holders. Period California stairwell is dotted with geometric tiles on terracotta pavers along with an understated wrought iron stair rail, original to this 1930s home.

Blue skies, rolling waves, sun, sand and sea. Its no wonder California's boosters had such an easy time convincing people to visit or move to the Golden State. Mural by Taylor Tilery, Los Angeles, California, c1934-1938; contemporary iron frame with palm tree accent.

Taylor Tilery of Santa Monica ventured north to San Francisco to depict the famous Golden Gate Bridge and an airplane in flight, c1930s. Vintage six-tile mural in hand wrought iron frame.

Impressive entry shows off California plein aire artist Marion Kavanaugh Wachtel (1870-1954), in an oil landscape in its original frame with engraved artist stamp. Vintage Hispano Moresque tile bench, with scrolled iron. The Gladding McBean vintage fountain piece represents a cherub riding a turtle in classic turquoise glaze. Pair of carved wood Chinese foo dogs, c1800.

Colorful home office wall displays California plein aire paintings and is dotted with Arts & Crafts oak, vintage tile displays from Taylor and D. & M., and ceramics from Gladding McBean, Bauer, and Catalina as well as ceramic artist Barbara Willis. Early monk bookends by Gladding McBean in foreground were made concurrently with Rufus Keeler's tenure at GMB, Malibu Pottery, and Catalina Island Pottery, although in differing sizes and glazes.

Panoramic vintage photo of Avalon Harbor, Catalina Island, California, 1920s.

Birds and Other Creatures

Inspiration from nature and her creatures was a major focus of California tile and pottery makers. Catalina led the way, but Taylor was the most prolific in this subject manner. Parrots, dragons, frogs, storks, and chickens, represent only a small fraction of the wide range of imaginative designs produced in the Golden State.

Deco style wood table base inset with four-tile roundel of pheasant and branches on black background by Taylor Tilery. Unusual, thick, black-glazed lamp by Catalina Island Pottery. The design for the hand painted parchment lampshade was inspired by Catalina's *Memorial* tile, whose tiles were made specifically for the Wrigley Botanical Gardens in Avalon.

Three vintage tile bird murals. Left and back: double parrots and jaybirds by Taylor Tilery. Foreground: birds of paradise by D. & M. All in original wood tables.

Taylor Tilery double parrot panel with rare buff color background and matte finish in wood table.

Grouping of vintage tile bird murals with vintage wood bases. Top left is attributed to Tudor and shows small birds with flowers and trim. On the right and in the foreground are two Taylor Tilery tables, plumed birds of paradise, and three lime green and orange parrots with colorful flowers.

Taylor bird murals featuring a single parrot on left and pheasants on right. A Tudor mural with a small bird is in back. Some of the flora and fauna themes executed in tile were created and shared by tile artists and manufacturers of the period, in part because employees and artists moved from company to company and often took their designs and/or glazes with them.

Stylized parrots on black background attributed to Tudor. The attractive and sturdy oak table base has an interesting crossbar.

Uncommon vanilla color background in round tile table, with mural featuring large beautiful bird and branches is attributed to Taylor. Six-tile mural of flying and perching parrots is attributed to American Encaustic Tile.

Close view of same flying and perching parrots mural with black background, in six-tile wooden tray top table, attributed to American Encaustic Tile, Hermosa Beach, CA..

Prolific and diverse, scores of California tile companies utilized ceramists and designers during the 1920s-30s to create a great number of colorful murals designed for the home. Birds were a popular subject, as is shown here in an abstract bird mural by Taylor Tilery in hand hammered iron frame with copper corners.

This protected porch makes a fine display area for four of the six bird murals by Catalina Island, c1928, in wrought iron framework. Pale olive green board and batten walls of contemporary California ranch home provide a neutral backdrop. From left to right, double parrots, green single parrot, toucans and lorikeets. Bauer oil jar in cobalt blue and yellow ribbed Garden City flowerpot flank vintage metal patio chair.

Catalina Island Pottery produced only a small number of scenic murals during their early years and their works are among the most sought after and difficult to find today. Shown are small single parrot head table with original iron deco base and *Crested Crane* tile set, in original wood table base, c1930.

Catalina Island Pottery produced only six unique bird murals designed by their resident artists (all California listed artists). Their most likely inspiration was the popular "Bird Park." This single, red parrot six-tile set with borders, in original carved wood radio cabinet, is found in both a green and a red version.

Catalina collectors have, when necessary, created their own names for the bird murals. This one is known as the *Fantasy Bird*. All Catalina bird murals are in vertical format and "six tiles make the bird," borders are two by six inches. Shown here in island-designed iron frame. Note: Taylor Tilery made many more bird sets than Catalina and so Taylor is often mistakenly (perhaps with a tad of wishful thinking) identified as Catalina.

Catalina Island *Crested Crane* mural and border tile with island-designed iron frame. New collectors should be aware that these designs have been reproduced in recent years and if seeking a vintage set must take care to guarantee that tiles are authentic and old. (See *Collecting California* section.)

Catalina *Double Parrot* mural and borders tile with island design iron frame.

Vintage *Toucans* with borders and island design iron, Catalina Island Pottery. "Tookie" the toucan was the mascot of the Catalina Bird Park.

Uncommon *Lorikeets* or *Parakeets* mural and borders by Catalina Island. Iron frame is island-designed.

Catalina *Single parrot* mural in red, with borders set into wrought iron frame.

Kissing parrots plate in turquoise on red clay. This is the smaller of two sizes at eight inches diameter. Catalina Island Pottery.

Catalina's Bird Park was established in the winter of 1929 by William Wrigley Jr. as a free amenity for all visitors to the "Magic Isle." Shown are original bird park tiles salvaged from the park when it was closed in the 1960s. The entrance area still stands on the Island and there are enough vintage tile installations in Avalon to warrant both a visit and its nickname "The Tile Isle."

Close view of Malibu Potteries "signature" on bottom of monk bookends marked with the date 1926. (See *Bibliography* for further reading.)

Dramatic Malibu Potteries Persian design tile mural with double facing peacocks, urns, and foliage. Eighteen tiles set in contemporary iron floor stand to allow for easy movement.

Gathering of single bird image tiles by Malibu and Calco with soft matt glazing, set in similar custom iron frames. Ceramic genius Rufus Keeler (1885-1934) ran both companies in the 1920s and 1930s after a stint at Gladding McBean. Tiles of this type were made by a number of California artisans in the 1920s-1940s, which can make it challenging to tell them apart. High quality reproductions also make it hard to tell old from new. Consult California tile reference books for identification help. Pricing can vary greatly and when it comes to any antique, it's always "buyer beware," so do your homework.

Historic Malibu display with single *kissing parrots* tile, their Monk bookends, peacock mantle tile, and a scarce salesman's sample box, along with a Batchelder ashtray, and a Calco mantel bird tile, all atop Monterey oval racetrack table.

Elaborate Claycraft (1921-1939) parrot and flower mural contains fifty tiles and embellishes a shady garden wall. Contemporary heavy hand made twisted iron frame.

Pictorial rooster and hen plaque in Brayton Laguna's signature color glazes, which were developed by Durlin Brayton in the 1920s, in a generous 11" diameter size. Signed in clay, and pencil dated 1942, with built-out notches on back to aid in hanging.

Catalina Island Pottery, artist-painted plate showing colorful cock fighting image. Intricate period wrought iron frame surrounds 10" plate. Almost all Catalina artist-painted plates were executed on white glazed backgrounds in "cold paint." Note that the term "cold painted" is very different than "glazed" or "glaze painted" (see *Terminology* section).

San Jose Workshop pictorial cock fighting mural shows well on a white background glaze. Two 8" tiles make the scene in this contemporary iron hanger.

Close view of early Catalina Island Pottery frog bookends, showing an Arts and Crafts influence, made of heavy clay and sometimes not marked. One of a pair in Descanso green.

Three little clay flower frogs by Bauer Pottery, in early stoneware glazes of blue and green from the 1930s, sit in a clover
leaf candy dish by Catalina Island Pottery in Toyon red glaze
on Monterey hand painted floral bookshelf.

Catalina Toyon red tobacco jar sans lid has raised design
scroll, shown with California Bear red clay bookend by Bauer
on Monterey bookshelf with "rosemaling" style florals.

Watercolor rendering of a tile installation for the
Webb School in Claremont by Henry Krier. Mr. Krier, a
top tile installer based in Monrovia, California, in the
1920s-1940s designed this mosaic tile water fountain
along with many other famous installations in the
state. This rendering survived along with a few others
and was subsequently matted and framed.

Monterey bench in old wood finish with keyhole shaped cutouts and superb iron detail by
Mason Manufacturing. Custom pieces were
made by Monterey to order. Next to the bench
is a dainty Monterey end table in old wood
finish with florals. Surrounding the bench
is assortment of Gladding McBean garden
and fountain pieces in the sometimes drippy,
turquoise signature glaze. The plump redhead
has been extensively trained to perch *near*
pottery not *on* it.

Floral and Geometric

Whether Moorish, Deco, Tunisian, Mayan, Persian, Hispano Moresque, or Japanese, design influences in tile have strong artistic and historic roots. Tile artists in California during its Golden Era studied ancient methods and styles and took their work very seriously. The collector today has many makers, design techniques, and forms to consider.

Once a Catalina table, now sans base, this nine tile set is reused as a circular wall hanging showing orange poppies on rich Chinese yellow glaze. Consider your vintage tile pieces as ceramic "paintings" or color accents. Some images look better on the wall vertically than on a table horizontally. Imperial radio cabinet holds vintage mini-saltillo with grouping of four Catalina Island Pottery pieces in turquoise glaze.

Catalina Island vintage tile top tables with original island-produced iron bases. Left: Wrigley *Memorial* tiles in a deco base; rear: round poppy design; right: hexagon poinsettia design.

Taylor Tilery produced this California poppy set, the state flower, in vivid orange buds and flowers on a black background. Fifteen inches across, not including the poppy accent, contemporary iron frame, custom made by local blacksmith.

Bouquet of Catalina Island Pottery tile tables include single color matte green circular set (back left), octagonal red set (back right), floral sets (front left and right), single decorative tile center set (back center), and black and yellow Moorish sets (front center). Original Island made wood and iron bases.

Floral themed tile tables in original turned wood bases by: Santa Monica Brick (parent company of Taylor Tilery): octagonal tile set (rear); Taylor *California Poppies* (front left); and octagonal set attributed to Taylor (front right). Dark wood finish and leather back strap on signed Monterey desk chair.

Floral themed tables in original hand wrought iron bases. The table at the back left, by Santa Monica Brick (1923-1940), contains sixteen 5" tiles. The remaining tables are by Hispano Moresque: Persian tile set (right rear) with integrated decorative borders; four tile floral by designer Harry Hicks with plain borders (front left); the table at the front right shows same floral tile shards in concrete. Bauer ringware flowerpot in orange.

1930s Catalina floral tiles form a planter cube lined with concrete. (*Photo courtesy of Bill Noonan.*)

Large vintage Malibu circular tile patio table with star center, utilizing an array of tile designs and colors set in Spanish Revival-style iron base.

Two Malibu Pottery vintage tile tables with floral motifs. Left: a colorful approach in four large format tiles in an iron base; right: a more dramatic black background in a wood and iron cross-bar Spanish Revival-style table.

Malibu Potteries was known more for tile than actual pottery pieces, of which there were relatively few. Shown at left is a tea tile designed for use as a trivet. Beside it are two versions of their Moorish plates, which show a deep recessed technique with a noticeable raised line separating the six or more glaze colors. Center plate is thirteen inches across, and one at the right measures six inches.

Geometric design tiles in various patterns by Taylor Tilery and (far right) D. & M. Colorful and useful whether in wood or iron any of these could be used for a side, coffee, or patio table. Keep your vintage tile tables out of direct sunlight and out of heavy rain or freezing weather to protect their finish, if possible.

D. & M. octagon table in an unusual vintage iron base. Iron-base tables were originally designed for outdoor use and often have some rusting or wear from the elements. Today, these tables are used indoors and out. If desired, iron bases can be darkened with stove black or dark furniture stain and steel wool.

Taylor, Tudor, and D. & M. geometric tile tables in authentic signed Monterey and (far right) Imperial bases. Monterey used California tile from many makers and set them into their bars, tables, desks, smoke stands, and dressers to create some of the more sought after Monterey pieces.

Heraldic D. & M. table shows griffons and shields in an authentic iron base.

Catalina griffon paver tile made of terra cotta, shows recessed glaze technique. *(Photo courtesy of Bill Noonan.)*

Mosaic, Patchwork, and Shards

Santa Monica Tile Company was known for their deep relief cuenca stylized tiles shown here on an original factory "sampler" tabletop.

D. & M. sampler table uses small 4" tiles to show off many of their patterns, shown here on an interesting notched and twisted iron base. These exact tile patterns can be found in two larger sizes and other vintage makers, as well as contemporary tile artists, show these designs in similar versions.

This unusual Tudor and yellow Catalina tile mosaic coffee table works well inside or out.

Raised fireplace hearth uses vintage tile combinations and shard pieces in broken tile mosaic technique for this recent installation. Broken tiles on hearth and entrance in this home are traditional for "keeping out bad spirits."

Mosaic Hillside flower pot made from ringware bowl shards pressed into red concrete shares this front ranch style porch with a large Catalina hand coiled oil jar, Catalina spittoon, and Gladding McBean cache pot, along with a three 8" tile San Jose Workshops agave mural in original iron surround.

D. & M. tile shard steps were laid in concrete when this home was built in 1928. The entire patio is ringed with the same pattern and this outdoor living area also boasts an original matching tile fountain.

This homeowner found a creative way to use old tiles, plates, and a full tile set inset into an entrance pathway. There are many ways to incorporate vintage tiles into remodeling projects, and it's a great way to recycle broken, cracked or chipped tiles if it doesn't make financial sense to repair them. Make sure you're certain of your vintage tile's value before permanently installing.

CALIFORNIA REVIVAL:

DETAILS

Tile and Paint Touches

Inventive use of real and faux tile techniques can provide just the right accent to finish off a wall, a floor, or a wainscoting, no matter which room of the house. Painted accents and custom designs add interest and complete the California look.

Vintage tile installation utilizes "river of life" border tiles to transition from the orange floor to the black wainscoting. By studying old techniques one can find ways to use vintage style in new installations.

Example of a new tile installation in a kitchen using vintage techniques. An offset geometric tile border is used with bold field tiles for a backsplash.

Reproduction tile backsplash adds vintage flare with Batchelder tile bird motif "dots."

Original vintage tiles in a 4" size "dot" the stairway risers in this home. Staircases provide various opportunities to use reproduction tiles for a vintage look.

Period impressed concrete stairs risers give a tile feeling with differing floral motifs for a tone on tone look.

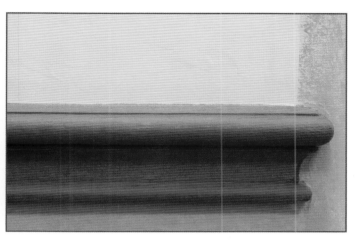

Faux wainscoting tiles are accomplished with skillful paint and plaster for an inventive "terra cotta" ledge in this family's remodeled great room.

Reproduction tile "dots" enliven a brick pathway.

Custom wainscoting achieved via hand painted sombrero and swirl paint design on textured wall.

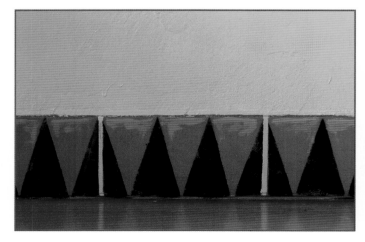

Painted faux tile has maximum effect in this floor trim. Built up border is painted to look like tiles down to the faux grout lines.

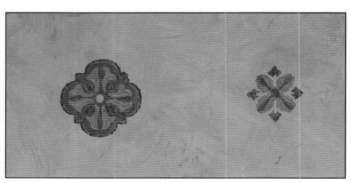

Tile-like stencils "brand" this bright wall in Catalina-style, the work done by a contemporary artist.

Elaborate and stylized stencils and recent hand painted designs give a tile-like appearance to this entranceway.

Another tile touch in paint uses three colors to achieve the look of a single tile on this stucco wall.

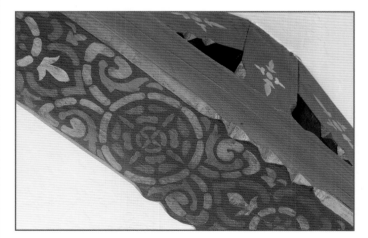

Contemporary stenciled ceiling beams echo the European rosemaling techniques used by painters in the 1920s.

Collection Display

From super-collector to novice, California aficionados are passionate about showing off their "finds." Whether simplistic or extreme, collecting "one of everything in every color," or a pristine one-of-a-kind example, your display options range from expensive vintage cabinetry, custom designed pieces, flea market finds, to big-box store bookcases. No matter what the framework, lighting and placement should be given top priority in the planning phase.

Vintage Bauer store sign in chartreuse glaze. Bauer Pottery (1910-1962) is most known for its brightly colored ring dinnerware in the 1930s, which reflected the popular patio culture of the day.

Bauer chartreuse *Moderne* and *La Linda* forms include a swan planter and wood-topped canisters from the 1960s. These styles crossover from modern design work well no matter what your architecture.

Bauer ringed flowerpots in graduated sizes share a built-in nook with Mexicana figures and wooden photo albums from the 1930s.

Bauer and Catalina share a glass fronted spice cabinet that holds salt and peppers, creamers, and sugars in various forms and sizes.

Vivid Bauer ringed cylinder vases line a kitchen window and provide a color reference for the walls and a contrast to the contemporary red tile countertop.

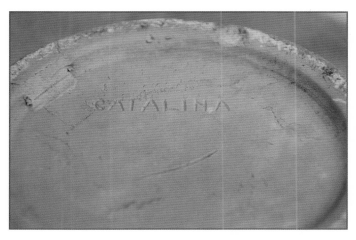

A Catalina Island mark on the bottom of a huge garden pot. Catalina (1926-1936) had many unique ways of signing their myriad pottery pieces but they are usually either iron stamped or etched in the mold. People frequently misread these as hand etched signatures. If it reads "pottery" and not either "Catalina Island," "Catalina Isle," or "Catalina Island Pottery," it's from Gladding McBean on the mainland and is not Island-made.

Bauer ringed Spanish pots, Matt Carlton vases, and a desert-themed Catalina painted plate, share a media "pocket" cabinet tucked inside a dividing wall. When building, the owners made sure there were adequate nooks and crannies above, below, and within the structural elements of the home in which to display their collections.

This custom contemporary Catalina Island home's entry hallway uses a double alcove built specifically for display of large forms such as oil jars and heavy garden pots. Integrated lighting adds drama from overhead and the deep recess allows collection display while keeping it out of the way of foot traffic.

Catalina oil jar looks triple nice in this specially designed bathroom niche over the sink. The tile surrounds are vintage style contemporary and the wooden base is recent.

A Monterey-style hutch attributed to Del Rey (see *Terminology*) with hand painted flowers enlivens a contemporary condominium on Catalina Island. Shown is another example of grouping by color with different forms of Catalina on each shelf. Contemporary oil painting features the Sombrero fountain in Avalon and the iron-base tile and ashtray set is vintage Malibu.

Imperial corner cabinet has display above and storage below. Made in the 1930s of mahogany, as opposed to Monterey's alder wood, many of Imperial's designs were directly copied from Monterey although with slightly different sizing. Display shows each shelf with a different color of Catalina Island pottery, blue, red, and experimental brown, with top shelf holding cold-painted (see *Terminology*) vintage coasters featuring birds at the famous bird park, which was executed by an as-yet-unknown artist on the Island. These were made as tourist items prior to 1937, and are being reproduced today. Large Catalina seafoam oil jar in original wooden base.

Large Monterey corner cabinet has room both in and on top. Interior features Catalina blue glazed pieces, small San Jose Workshop plates, and vintage silver. Top holds Catalina floral line vases in various colors.

An oak lawyer's bookcase is another way to show off a collection of Catalina pottery and tile rarities. There's a mix of colors and themes with black, white and brown, as well as blue with yellow accents. Glass doors pull down to protect from dust while still allowing a full view.

Glassed-in oak display case allows for a mix of books, pottery and tile and displays a historic selection of pieces by Bauer, Pacific, Garden City, Brayton, Malibu and Catalina. Notice the Garden City flowerpots lining the top in all glaze colors.

Overhead wall shelving in dark finish with white and ivory glazed Catalina Island vases in a guest room with a mono-chromatic theme. This often overlooked display choice is an easy one with contemporary and easy-to-install shelves that can work in any style home, especially when space is at a premium. Sepia-toned vintage photos complete the look.

Catalina lamp and undersea plaque, and various pottery pieces rest on top of large, oversized wraparound cabinets in this home office, drawing the eye upwards. Lucite plat-forms help to vary height and the crown molding frames the display.

Catalina- filled contemporary eye-level cabinets with stark white background and glass shelves allow built in lighting to shine on all levels of this collector's museum quality treasures. Glass doors can be left open or closed.

Built-in shelf over the breakfast bar window allows large Cellini Craft vintage tile platters to rest there. Contemporary yellow tile on bar, Monterey rattan woven and wood chairs with original painting.

Cabinet top display shows Catalina Pottery figurines designed by Dorr Bothwell in terra cotta and glaze, as well as a Catalina artist-painted plate, and a Deco coffee pot in blue with green lid. Often collectors will mix different makers with similar themes. Many Catalina Island pottery collectors also collect the Gladding McBean mainland-made Catalina Pottery items (see *Terminology* section).

Catalina blue shows well against dark Mission style oak. Small oil jar form, "Goofy" goat, Swastika vase (an ancient Indian symbol of good luck), and a period Avalon flying fish graphic cigarette lighter.

A museum style display cabinet with a Calco tile base sits in this study/home office and features historic California pottery and tile makers from the "Golden era" representing Bauer, Pacific, Vernon Kilns, Metlox, Catalina, Tudor, Malibu, Poxon, Stockton, Padre, Ra-Art, and Cemar, among many others. Many collectors seek out the lesser-known makers, and can sometimes find good bargains.

An oak flat filing cabinet, the type used by architects, is repurposed for tile display and is excellent for showcasing single tile examples, curiosities, or ephemera.

A trio of tile renderings done in watercolor by tile designer Henry Krier, Monrovia, California, in the 1930s and 1940s. Also on display on this red Monterey desk is Mr. Krier's personal mosaic board with tiny tile pieces made by Batchelder.

A single example of one of Catalina's most enduring forms, called the *step* vase, in Descanso green showing brown under glaze "burn." Other makers copied this form, although unmarked and in smaller sizes.

Catalina *step* vases and candle votives repeat in twelve out of approximately thirteen Catalina glaze colors, including blended glaze (not an experimental glaze although sometimes called so) and rare black. Repeated forms in multiples make for an impressive display.

Brayton Laguna's colorful dinnerware has a hand crafted rustic quality. Brayton was among the first to bring a mix and match approach to casual California dining.

Rare Catalina scout lamps and table lamps share a countertop with their Bauer cousins' handled Rebekah vases. Comical Monterey painting shows a character losing a grip on his horse. Shades are reproductions taken from vintage Catalina designs.

Monterey Furniture
A California Original

Vintage postcard from the Mayflower Hotel in downtown Los Angeles features signed art from the mysterious Monterey painter. His comic character, in his trademark hat, is on the right with a buddy. The original version of this painting hung in the hotel's "Monterey Cocktail Room," where George Mason said his staff did some moonlighting (Dempster interview).

Discovery

Years ago when pondering a furniture style that worked for her 1960s ranch home that didn't involve plastic and Plexiglas, a homeowner in Northern California discovered an unusual sofa and chair sitting in a junk shop's side yard. They didn't look like Mission oak; in fact they were made of Oregon alder. They had a casual look with a rope seat but the floral decoration gave them a vaguely Mexican flare. They were either the worst or the best things she'd ever seen, so she took them home, lived with them and hoped for the best, when something unexpected happened. They really grew on her. They were fun pieces, with good proportions, very well designed, really comfortable, with burnt-in horseshoe brands. She asked the question that passionate Monterey collectors always seem to ask once they get hooked. Who the heck made this furniture and where could she get more?

She had found Monterey furniture, rustic and painted, true California originals made in Los Angeles beginning in 1929, sold at high end stores all over the country during the style's glory years, the 1930s, but in intervening decades left out to rot on many a porch, or in this case at a junk shop.

Luckily the story had a happy ending despite the dealer's misinformation, "This is Monterey Mission furniture, you see, made at the Mission in Monterey. Someone put all this paint and flowers all over it, so you should strip that all off to get it dark like it was originally." At the whopping price of one hundred and fifty dollars for sofa and chair it was the kind of story collectors, hopeful of Monterey treasure, loved to hear. Today select pieces with original finishes and hard-to-find forms can command tens of thousands of dollars. As a skeptical friend asked, "So let me understand this, the more you know the more you pay?" Better stated, the more you know the more confident you are to step up and buy the right piece at the right price, even a high one.

The Backstory

In 1929 Mason Manufacturing Company on East 60th in downtown Los Angeles was in the business of making patio furniture and lighting when they were approached by designers at Barker Brothers, then the leading department store in Southern California. The building boom in Spanish style homes had left an unmet need in the market; there were Spanish Revival reproduction furniture styles on the market, but nothing with a rugged "Out West" feel that would be suitable for use in these interiors. Movies of the time increased the public's interest in a nostalgic and romanticized past. Founder Frank Mason's son George, who served as the company designer, sales-

man, and one-man PR firm, quickly whipped up a line of chairs, sofas, tables, and a wonderful marriage was made. Produced from 1929 to 1943, Monterey, with a constantly expanding and innovative line exclusive to Barker Brothers in Southern California, became much more than just a regional trend. Spanish style homes were popping up throughout California, and in Florida, Chicago, Arizona, and New Mexico (albeit with a Southwestern flare). Monterey was carried by high-end department stores across the country including Gumps, Emporium Capwell, Hales, and Bullocks Wilshire, sometimes with the name *Ranch-0*.

Excerpt from 1933 Catalog entitled "Monterey Furniture created by Barker Brothers"

"Monterey furniture created by Barker Bros. for California Homes: In response to the persistent demand for furniture adapted to modern California architectural development yet moderate in cost, Barker Bros. created Monterey. At first only living room pieces were designed but the call for furnishings for the whole house has led to the creation of an entire Monterey ensemble. Bedrooms, dining rooms, living rooms, patios and gardens may now be furnished completely and delightfully in this early California manner. Rugs, draperies, lamps, china and decoratives in perfect harmony have been assembled. A whole house can be a well-planned ensemble in furniture of the same inspiration as the architecture itself.

Monterey furniture may be had in old red, straw ivory, Spanish green—all richly antiqued—

fects may be achieved through the combination of as many of these finishes as desired with a result at once arresting, spirited and above all, entirely livable.

Monterey Furniture Today

The California Revival approach to using Monterey in decor differs from a strictly purist approach. Monterey was "made to mix" and was always intended to complement other existing household furniture elements such as wicker, Victorian, or mission. Today we blend Monterey colors, finishes, and styles, along with contemporary leather sofas, modern classics, as well as Arts and Crafts and Golden Age California decor, or quality reproductions, which seems more in the spirit of what was originally intended than an all dark Arts and Crafts approach. Just like Catalina Island Pottery, which doesn't have to be red clay in order to be "good" or rare, judging the beauty of any specific piece of Monterey is in the eye of the beholder. The only exceptions are the last years of production, which took a detour away from the California look towards an American Colonial style. Even if marked, these pieces are less desirable to mainstream collectors at the current time. Western pieces of later vintage are great for use in cabins, lodges, and homes looking for a cowboy touch. Monterey used various finishes and made items to order throughout the life of the company. Their classic period pieces were still made at the end of the company's life for Camp Pendleton sometime during the lead up to America's involvement in World War II (1939-1941).

Many Monterey collectors display Catalina Island Pottery as a go-along with Monterey, and for good reason. Not only do they look great together, there are many intriguing Catalina-Monterey connections, deserving of further study. Although a time machine or a séance might be helpful, some evidence has come from oral histories and families of former employees. The one notable exception in groundbreaking new information has been the recent discovery of a historic Wrigley-Renton correspondence from that era shared by DM Renton's grandson David. The *Catalina Island Pottery and Tile Shop* on Olvera Street in Los Angeles, displayed all their wares on Monterey furniture. Both Monterey and Catalina appealed to the movie stars of the day, and George Mason was a handsome young man who was friends with most of them from his years at Hollywood High School. George spent a lot of time on Catalina both as a boy, with his family, and as a young man. He even told one collector that the painted finishes on Monterey were inspired by the California pottery colors. Catalina's matt glazes might be a top contender for this claim, especially since Catalina pre-dated Monterey's production by at least two years (Dempster interview). The holy grail of Catalina collecting is Monterey's Prohibition Bar topped with red and black Catalina field tiles, and one of the Catalina colors is even called "Monterey Brown."

The Great Depression followed by the War brought a change in decorating tastes, and the death of Frank Mason in 1944 brought the company's time to an end. Monterey's huge diversity of designs and finish treatments is one of the reasons that collectors have so much fun looking for that next special piece. Some sofas have built-in magazine racks, lamps grow out of bookcases, and table/lamp combinations are too numerous to describe. Frank Mason's partner even complained that George was changing the designs so much that they couldn't keep their production up (Dempster interview). One time George overheard a family that was looking longingly at the Barker Brothers Monterey display window. The children wanted Monterey, but the father said the furniture was too big for their house. So George made up a line of smaller sized chairs, tables, and sofas. (Dempster interview). Some of the best pieces have iron, but some great pieces have none. Original paint is always desirable, whether floral or Mexicana themed. A little wear and paint loss are acceptable but should not read as "shabby." Using a mix and match approach to decorating with Monterey, and using the best pieces you can find, no matter what their period, can enliven a room and represent the best use of the form.

Highly desirable Monterey pieces—bars, dressers, side tables, smoking stands, and buffets—are tile-topped, primarily with Hispano Moresque tiles, but D. & M., Taylor, and Catalina (see above) were also used.

Reproduction Monterey is being made today by various manufacturers and can cost close to the pricing for vintage pieces since it requires time-consuming hand work in wood, iron, and finishes. Some collectors and dealers repaint or refinish original branded Monterey furniture to achieve a vintage look, but pricing for these pieces is less than for original or pristine condition pieces. When it is strictly necessary to repair or replace a totally worn finish, stripping can be done, but sanding destroys the detailed marks and feel of the furniture and detracts greatly. Consult a professional and make sure to see examples of their work to ensure the best results. Prices on furniture and accessories vary greatly depending on the originality and condition of the finish, the style, rarity, where the item is purchased, and from whom. Dealing with reputable specialists in the area provides some degree of confidence, but if in doubt, ask for a written description of the item being purchased and inspect it carefully. There are many different makers of vintage Monterey *style* furniture such as: Imperial, made by the Imperial Cabinet Company of Los Angeles, known for its heavily hammered, thick ironwork and mahogany wood; Coronado, made by the Angelus Furniture Company, utilizing floral painting and rope trim: Del Ray, with its distinctive wooden spindles: and others that have become collectible in their own right. Imperial sometimes has sticker identification, Coronado is often branded with its name, and others are not marked. Most but not all Monterey is uniquely signed with a burnt-in horseshoe brand, and/or the burnt words "Monterey," so check this book and others carefully to study the subtle differences.

Monterey used many different styles of floral painting, some with thick applications of paint, some with Swedish-looking designs, Mexican floral, and Deco floral. Some of the painting resembles Rosemaling or Norwegian rose painting that incorporates crosshatching, a technique that likely came from the female Chouinard Art students that were employed at the plant (George Mason even attended the school for a brief time). Sometimes the artists would get bored with copying a certain style over and over, and were allowed to improvise with some wonderful results. In later years George and his wife would disagree about what kind of flowers they really were: she said "Rosemailing," he said "Spanish" (Connors interview). Ceiling beams painted by listed California artist Ejnar Hansen (1884-1965) and Peter Nielsen grace the Adamson House-Malibu Museum and are another influence on decorative painters of the time. The Mexican floral and folk art painted pieces are very prized today, and were top sellers in the 1930s.

Monterey's Mexican folk art painting style includes cartoon painting on boards with recurring characters (which in the context of the day were not deemed stereotypical) and are sometimes signed with an illegible signature currently called "Juan Intenoche" (see *Terminology*). They range from chili peppers, donkeys, horses, bulls, and people, to moody Mission scenes. George Mason wasn't crazy about the comic paintings, but the market seemed to go for it (Connors, interview). They were done in series, like animation frames or cartoon panels, in a black outline graphic style, which makes sense when you consider that the mystery painter who created them was said to be an animator, and we do know that his ideas and expertise allowed him to become head of Mason's painting department. Like many bosses he may have signed or approved other copies of his designs. Some Monterey paintings are not signed and do appear to be works by other artists and their quality varies greatly. (Visit www.findingjuanintenoche.com or our blog for more information.)

Painted Western motifs show cowboys, cactus, saddles, longhorns, and Mexican figures. Sometimes designs, or even the "Monterey" signature, were tooled into leather, and donkeys are a recurrent theme impressed into some chair backs. Leather was used not only for upholstery, but applied to tabletops with rawhide strings, and as accents on screens and lamp bases. It was said that Mason monopolized the leather trade in Los Angeles to the point that if you wanted leather for anything you'd have to go through Mason to get it. They even tried a short-lived leather clothing line (Dempster interview).

Monterey painted finishes include Desert Dust, Spanish Green, Old Red, Straw Ivory, Mexican White (a light yellow), Blue (mainly on bedroom sets),Smoky Maple or Cinnamon (appears stained but is actually painted orange with a dark brown top coat), orange, and a two-tone light and brown

combination, with many other custom variations. The stained finishes are Old Wood, Dark, Maple, and medium Dark, and other custom stains. The wood of the furniture was intentionally distressed and the finishes were given a rich aged appearance, even when new. The metalwork iron straps, pulls, lampshades, and other accents were hand hammered, then stained or painted (black and orange being the most common colors) and the iron shop at Mason was under the able supervision of foreman Max Gebhardt.

Don Shorts and Dolores "Dee" Fischer are rightly credited as being pioneers in their discovery, recognition, and early research into Monterey furniture and Old California design. At an exhibition in 1985 at the California Heritage Museum (then the Santa Monica Heritage Museum) they displayed fine examples of this decor and were happily surprised to discover that designer George Mason was still living. George was amazed by all the attention being paid to the furniture that he had helped to bring to life so many years before and he stated simply, "Furniture for California living was the idea." It still is.

Early Monterey wingback chairs and floor lamp, dark flooring, beams, and window trim create a dramatic mood in this corner seating area.

Close view of Monterey wingback chair with rope webbing and metal strapping. Traditionally leather was used for seat coverings, although woven material works as well. Monterey floor lamp has reproduction shade and saltillo adds a touch of color.

Monterey serving cart with signed Monterey painting of bucking horse. Useful as a bar or for food service, the cart rolls into place. Desert Dust finish with red painted top and cut out for ice bucket. Topped with three original Monterey table lamps and a wooden photo album with a Monterey caricature painting. Bauer ringware beverage service sits on a tile and plant saucer topped holder to left.

Imperial mini bar with Catalina tile top and hand painted fighting rooster detail set against a bright green wall. Malibu Moorish plates above, Catalina ringed flower pots in original Monterey stand left, and also in Catalina Island stand right

Monterey desk cabinet and chair have wood turned leg details typical of high quality pieces. Small concrete bears and bark canoes add a rustic touch. Paintings are Monterey, signed by the artist and are found in numbered sequences. These examples vividly show the artist's training in animation. On the right is the before image; to the left is the action scene.

Monterey green finish tall cabinet and chair create an extra display area in a long hallway. In the foreground is a Bauer oil jar in iron stand. Saltillos, Taylor wall murals, and Catalina Toyon red ball lamp.

Monterey tile-topped cellaret in dark finish has a secret sliding top, an ideal design feature for storing liquor bottles during prohibition. Dancing nymphs wall mural attributed to Dec-Art holds Bauer flowerpots. Spanish dancer figurine is European.

Using odd rather than even numbered groupings, such as these three Taylor wall murals, makes for a more pleasing display.

Dramatic Monterey buffet with starburst floral door fronts looks at home in this California Hacienda approach. Deep persimmon wall color sets off the other Spanish fixtures, yet mixes well with the vintage California tile bird scenes framed in iron.

Traditional Spanish Revival 1930s home has a formal dining room perfect for this long Monterey dining table and chairs. Carved Mexican bas relief wood panels are actually repurposed doors from the period. Simple lines and decor, including the Hillside Pottery flowerpot made of concrete and tile, give a stark clean look to the room.

Another view shows this traditional period home with minimal decor. Monterey library table at picture window, Hillside pot, Bauer ringed flowerpots in graduated sizes in twin niches. Color accents of yellow are echoed in stenciled ceiling and draperies.

Right:
Red Monterey slant top desk and rope webbed side chair, and desk lamp. Monterey did many custom painted finishes from bright to dull red, light to dark green, various shades of blue, white, yellow, and even orange. Customers could order the furniture painted to more correctly match their other furnishings, as Monterey's motto was "Made to mix." Be aware of re-painted and re-done finishes and make sure to see them in person prior to purchase.

Monterey desk with Taylor tile top in dark finish, with floral painted stool and Catalina Island vases in Toyon red. Contemporary cacti watercolors by local artist Robert Benson.

Monterey dining and/or desk chairs come in a wide variety of sizes and shapes. Many are variations on a theme, and most are marked with a horseshoe brand. Left: Monterey arm chair with embossed donkey on seat back; center: orange floral painted side table; right: camel back chair with hard woven seat. Pots are Bauer terra cotta Indian bowls.

Red Monterey dressing table brightens up a slate floored study. Three Catalina tile flowerpot wall hangers, Gladding McBean *Sailing to Catalina* mural, Malibu ship tile plaque. Monterey chair with Catalina tourist pillow.

Monterey dining sets came with four armless chairs and one armchair so gathering a matching set of six or more can be challenging. Most California Revival collectors prefer mixing and matching the Monterey finishes instead of a traditional dark only approach. Left to right: Monterey rush seat in light green, medium green with leather seat, unusual slotted back bench in dark, leather strap seat with metal backrest, light straw ivory paint on A-frame chair.

Dark finish Monterey slant back bucket chair at left, desert dust finish double slat back with leather strapped seat is center, and keyhole cellar chair at right. Concrete garden cactus and siesta man folk art pieces.

Left:
A Monterey bedroom suite shows red and dark finishes used together. Monterey bench in foreground, dark bed with iron scrollwork, side table with built-in lamp, red desk and chair in back corner. Large Monterey painting of a wild bullrider ties the look together.

Right:
Monterey A-frame dresser with Taylor Indian scout tile top has through-tenon detail on leg. Monterey mirror in red, hand painted desk lamp. Monterey used various California tiles to top their buffets, table bases, dining tables, dressers, and more.

Dark Monterey Gentleman's dresser and mirror with Catalina and Bauer red and black accents retains the bedroom's masculine look. Catalina Toyon red fishnet rope lamp.

Gold and brown hues lend an understated look to this young man's bedroom which features a Monterey double bed, bookcase, lounging chair, mirror, and painting, with one Bauer oil jar in foreground on Monterey chest.

Monterey tile-top buffet with matching Catalina Descanso green trophy lamps, and original vintage tile surround mirror. Although meant for the dining room, Monterey buffets are versatile and work in the entry, hallway, and bedrooms for storage and display.

Monterey bookcase, with crackle back and flowers, holds vintage Mexican folk art toys. Playful child's bucking bronco rocking chair in vinyl with tassels. This original Monterey painting is done in a painterly fashion using a romanticized versus comical style. Sold at Barker Brothers, Gumps, Hale's, Emporium Capwell, and Bullocks Wilshire, the finest department stores of their day—some paintings are signed but all are framed very distinctively. Be knowledgeable about recent reproductions.

Monterey corner cabinet holds Catalina blended glaze examples and bud vases, Garden City flowerpots, San Jose Workshops bookends, as well as tile and other curios. Large Catalina oil jars fit into stands originally made on the island at their blacksmith shop. The island iron shop also produced table bases; smoke stands, and many different styles of iron surrounds for plaques and pots.

Close view shows detail of Catalina Island bud vases in various glazes, Garden City flowerpots, Taylor 6" Caballero tile, and top center a reproduction Siesta Man bookend. (See book's web site for up to date *Resources.*)

Ironwork

California Revival style utilizes many types of metalworking in a wide variety of treatments indoors and out. Here we feature structural elements, entry and window treatments, as well as interior touches in lighting, plant stands, table bases, curtain rods, and some playful touches both from the Spanish Revival era and quality reproductions achieved by contemporary iron artisans. The tradition of blacksmithing has a long and valued history in California, and by showcasing some of the possibilities you can see for yourself what richness iron accents can add to your home.

Gates

Delicate custom ironwork gate matches original vintage fixtures on home and provides privacy for the back yard.

Elaborate custom iron scrollwork suits this elegant home entrance.

Seahorses floating in seaweed, painted aqua, enliven this whimsical, vintage, hand turned ironwork entry gate.

Simple triangles create a
pattern and repeat in this
lush garden's vintage gate.

Period Monterey-style wood and ironwork backyard gate centered
in archway uses a combination of heavy strapping and scrollwork
on the masonry perimeter wall.

Custom side entry gate leads beachgo-
ers to the backyard shower. Terra cotta
tile work uses reproduction Catalina tiles
for stair risers, and as "dots."

Spanish style entry bells decorate this home's front door.

Friendly custom garden gate keeps wandering dogs from the pathway but doesn't obstruct views in or out.

Vintage peacock bell ringer with elaborate pull-down handle shows fine period artistry.

Far left: Entry gate and vintage wall piece show similar ironwork and incorporate house numbers.

Left: Close view of iron street number sign.

Doors ,Windows & Balconies

Recessed front double door screen has period iron framework and is original to the home.

Elaborate iron bench and lighting fixture match the front door screen.

Detail of vintage iron bench shows turtle detail and repeating circle pattern.

This wood paneled front door features iron rosette touches and has custom grillwork with an iron rose designed by the owner.

Detail of iron rose and grill.

Courtyard double doors have hand turned wooden stiles and are backed by glass with twin wall sconces balanced on either side.

Red paver landing tiles and one simple iron drop lamp compliment the Spanish green kitchen and utility doors.

Moss green glass paneled doors lead from the flagstone patio to the living area. Unglazed Catalina floor vases provide a terra cotta counterpoint.

Close view of awning pole and crossbar.

Spanish green painted screen doors are topped by a matching awning with turned wrought iron poles.

An innovative custom iron and glass backed side entry door borrows from vintage design in its use of archways, recessed doors, and scrolling ironwork in this new California Revival style home.

Vintage iron gates can be repurposed indoors or out as shown in the placement of a hallway "door" in this vintage Spanish style home.

Quatrefoil shaped inserts in twin arched windows give a graceful old world touch to this breezeway.

Custom peek-a-boo iron grillwork allows light and view in an otherwise dark hallway.

Iron step out balcony curves gracefully up the wall and lends emphasis to the curved tile roofline.

Small iron window balcony adds emphasis, safety, and colorful plant display.

Custom wrought iron balustrade tops an upper stairwell for safety and beauty.

Scrolled iron balcony with a solid base off the master bedroom allows both pet and plants to perch.

Lighting and More

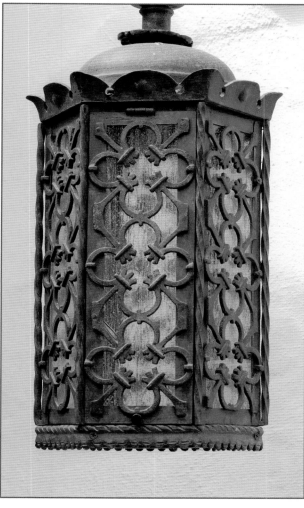

Close view of cast aluminum and ironwork. This technique was also used for some Malibu Pottery tile surrounds and table bases in the 1930s.

Mexican-style entry lantern has delicate features and a glass surround and is offset to one side of the ranch style door.

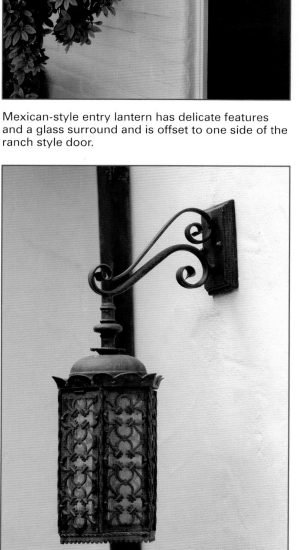

Left:
Vintage hanging cast aluminum, iron, and mica front door fixture hangs gracefully to one side of the front entrance to this classic Spanish Revival residence.

Right:
Formal large period Spanish entry lamp has fine detailing and uses an iron bar to keep it secure.

Another example of period cast aluminum, iron, and mica sconce used on an exterior wall.

Side entrance door with reproduction sconce, using a top center placement in this custom California Revival home.

Simple lines on this vintage porch sconce enhanced by golden mica.

Detail of reproduction sconce, which shows a jewel-toned stained glass technique.

Graceful vintage candle-style interior sconce casts dramatic light in this hallway.

This outdoor sconce features both Spanish and Mission styles and uses a center placement over the front door.

Period candle-style sconce is one of a pair that accents a dining room wall.

Decorative iron scrollwork details dot a bare hallway.

Double candle-style sconce with dramatic twisted base lights a stairwell.

Iron drapery hangers from the 1930s with added Malibu tile accents decorating each end.

Vintage wrought iron curtain hangers with dramatic floral flourish.

Rich detail on this iron drapery "shelf" is beautiful enough to be used with or without draperies.

Leaf and swirl details echo vintage ironwork.

Custom ironwork fireplace screen with delicate leaf detail inset and surrounded by hearth tiles.

Vintage ironwork keyhole and doorknob show incredible attention to detail.

Salvaged iron and mica dining room chandelier has vintage tile inserts along the sides.

Ornate twirling iron details on this vintage hanging fixture enliven a stairwell.

Combinations, Tile, Pottery and Iron

A combination of vintage tile and iron elements on this hall-way mirror show the subtle sophistication of 1930s design.

Tile wall planter uses simple iron, vintage Catalina tile, and a Bauer flowerpot. Travel magazine from the 1930s shows a graphic artists design that was used as the basis for a Gladding McBean wall mural. Artists of the day were often commissioned to create designs and scenic themes for depiction in tile.

Custom iron framework and reproduction tile is used to achieve a contemporary interpretation with Hispanic touches. Used in a sheltered outdoor location, it reflects a Mexican fountain in the courtyard.

Classic multicolored tile set attributed to Taylor Tilery was placed in tinted terrazzo and then framed in ironwork that includes potholders. This terrazzo and a concrete technique were used for both table bases and wall plaques and is a simple way to add color to a garden wall and achieve a California Revival effect.

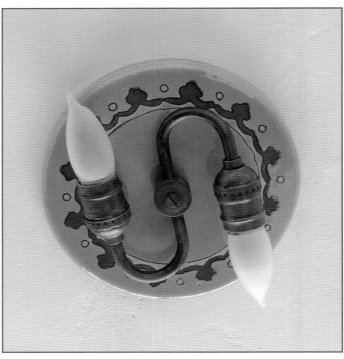

Round Malibu tile was created with a glazed center hole to allow for use as a doorbell, buzzer back plate, or in this case as a ceiling fixture.

Circular D. & M. tile lamp has hand-painted ironwork resembling cattails. It rests on a nine tile square bedside table by Taylor Tilery composed in a racetrack pattern.

Reproduction California-style tiles and borders are formed into a planter pot and rest in a custom iron stand, ideal for use around a sunny pool where reproduction tiles can stand the sun and elements.

Elegant Gladding McBean raised design oil jar's massive form shows well when slightly elevated, as on this stylized iron holder with griffon-like creatures holding rings.

Catalina Island pottery oil jar in seafoam glaze stands out when combined with a black, Island-made, wrought iron holder with center strap.

COLLECTING CALIFORNIA:
DECORATING IDEAS

Hardscape

Architecture—Spanish, Contemporary, Mediterranean, Cabin, Lodge, and Ranch Style homes all lend themselves readily to the California Revival style of decorating. English, Arts and Crafts, Modern, and Asian architecture can also accommodate the look using a little imagination. A recent issue of *Architectural Digest* featured a trendy newlywed's Manhattan apartment done up in vintage Monterey furniture with Mexican-styled appointments with great success.

Decorators—Using a professional decorator is a good thing if you're unsure of what you like, or if undertaking a large building project. Many people today choose an Interior Design consultant or an advisor but still enjoy finding vintage treasures that are meaningful to them to add into the mix. Resources for fabrics, furniture, and basics are not as restricted as they once were. Some of our featured homes used decorators, others preferred to do it themselves. Trust your instincts but recognize what you don't know, and where you need help.

Historic Homes—If you are lucky enough to be the guardian of a home with vintage California tile and architecture, treasure it and preserve it. It's rarely warranted to replace authentic vintage tile, from both a monetary and an aesthetic point of view, even if it shows some wear and tear. Realtors now advertise vintage tile as an important feature of homes for sale. Enjoy the color and vibrancy that the artists, designers, and architects have entrusted to you. Remodel wisely with a light hand. Use high quality reproduction art tiles in the California style where needed.

Paint—Coloring your exterior and interior walls and ceilings, in shades of white, putty, terra cotta, or stone will provide a neutral backdrop for the colorful pottery, tile, and textiles inside and outside your home. Many California collectors choose to limit colorful accent walls or floors.

Landscape—Some landscape designers today specialize in native California plants, and know how to work in the California genre, whether it's a Santa Barbara, Santa Monica, or a wine country look. Homeowners will find many more nurseries that now feature a California approach to planting as well, some with an emphasis on drought tolerance.

Outdoor Living—Wrought iron furniture, ironwork accents, garden pots, tile tables, fountains, and tile pathways, add richness to outdoor kitchens and rooms.

Furniture

Authenticate—Buy from reputable dealers who guarantee what they sell to be original and/or as described. Catalina "style" tile is not authentic vintage Catalina Island tile, just as Monterey "style" might not be branded Monterey. Ask lots of questions. Anecdotal information might be interesting, even if unverifiable (not *every* piece of Monterey came from a movie star's home, and not *every* tile table started life at the Riverside Mission Inn). "To the best of my knowledge" is not a guarantee but an educated guess, some times incorrect.

Backdrop—Consider using a neutral fabric palate on your furnishings, and your flooring. Then you can use colorful accessories and avoid busyness.

Combine—Simple forms sometimes look better with intricate pieces, and intricate pieces can work well in the more formal areas of your home: entry, living room, and dining room. Contrast works.

Display—Not every antique piece in a room needs to be of a single vintage. How you combine old treasures with new furnishings and accessories will enrich the look of your home while also reflecting your personality and interests. Mix Spanish baroque with modern art if that's what you like.

Groupings—Think of your rooms as paintings-and the whole home as a composition—and try not to be rigid about manufacturer or era. A family room shared by pets and kids needs furniture and upholstery that can stand up to the job. Mix and match forms and finishes to achieve a blended look rather than being too "matchy" by using all dark or all colored finishes.

Accents

Books—There are many books on vintage California furnishings, tile and pottery in your library or at bookstores. Research before you buy and learn the ins and outs of your area of interest to avoid making costly mistakes. Visit museums, shops, and web sites that specialize in California style.

Focus—Collect pottery or tile from two or three different vintage or reproduction makers *or* pick one or two forms from many makers. Find complimentary colors and choose pieces that work for your home, apartment, or display space.

Color—Color schemes can change from room to room. Use colors that compliment each other in groupings or in specific areas. An example: if you have a lot of orange pottery in a room, red furniture or fabrics, will clash unless in small doses.

Cost—Some coveted pieces can be very difficult and costly to acquire. Consider less discovered makers or items that are undervalued because of glaze color or condition. Set your own trends.

Groupings—Show off a collection if you have one, whether art or objects. Using pieces in "three's" or "five's" is a time-honored display technique.

Heirlooms—Use family heirlooms, fun souvenirs, ephemera, and memorabilia as featured pieces or to add character to newer furniture and architecture.

Forms—California pottery is an important element of decorating for the California Revival look. Decide what colors and forms appeal most to you before buying. Love small bud vases or large oil jars? Start by keeping your focus.

On-line—Where pricing is involved, on-line auctions and fixed price items can fluctuate greatly given participating bidders, time of year, and possible shill or fraudulent bidding. Check feedback carefully and don't believe everything you read. It can be the Wild West or a very satisfying experience but it's always "buyer beware."

Pricing—If you are serious about collecting, buy the best that you can afford. You'll always regret what you don't buy, not what you do. If you are careful about your purchases these collectible and historic pieces should continue to appreciate over the years.

Textiles—California Revival furnishings are enhanced by the use of a variety of subtle and ethnic textiles. Whether vintage or contemporary, either rich Spanish, or playful Mexicana, they can add a soft touch, bringing the mix of heavier tile, pottery, or iron elements into balance.

Texture—Textures are key to creating a unified look for your home inside and out. Avoid going overboard with one element or another. Consider heavy/light, rough/smooth, soft/hard, etc. and pick a few key elements to repeat to keep the mood consistent.

Use—Live with your collection. Put flowers in your vases, light the lamps, and serve on your dishes. Hand wash vintage plates, etc. and don't use them for food storage. Precious items that are extremely valuable can always be kept under glass. Oil jars can be filled with sand outdoors for anchoring, or used as fountain pieces if properly configured.

THE SPANISH REVIVAL MOVEMENT:
A BRIEF HISTORY

Missions

California author Cary McWilliams observed that things change in California more rapidly than in other states. In a relatively short historical framework Spanish explorers, Franciscan missionary colonizers, Native Americans, *Californios, Mexicanos,* Anglos, Chinese, multi-ethnics, and immigrants and treasure hunters of all nationalities influenced California culture through their beliefs and ideas. In 1769, fifty years after Franciscan friars from Spain established the Texas missions, Fr. Junipero Serra was sent to act as both church and state in "Alta California." Spain ruled over Mexico and wanted to secure their rights to this remote outpost before the Russians or the French could. It's hard to imagine how desolate and inhospitable the missionaries found the land to be. It was only through their efforts and determination (along with their Native American converts, most no more than indentured servants) that they were able to succeed in their conquest of the land and its indigenous peoples. The establishment of a 500-mile long chain of twenty-one mission compounds accomplished Spain's colonization of Alta California, the pacification and civilization (so-called) of the Native American population, the establishment of vast cattle ranches producing hides and tallow, and massive plantings of olives, grapes, and orchards. The missions did their job so well that they made themselves obsolete, and in 1834 the governor of California, (under Mexican rule since 1821) secularized the rich mission lands and vast herds for the *Californios* and *Mexicanos*, multi-ethnic Native Americans, ex-military men, and newly arrived settlers, who had long coveted the churches' rich properties. The Gold Rush in 1848 brought a new wave of immigrants, mainly Anglo, creating a huge population explosion, and when the dust of war settled in 1850, Mexico ceded ownership to the United States. The Huntington Library has just finished (in August 2006) an important Early California Population Project with a database detailing the up-until-now unknown facts of the lives and deaths of 110,000 people, mostly Native Americans, who lived in California at the twenty-one missions during the 18th and 19th centuries. Scholars, genealogy buffs, and interested writers will now have on-line access to the California history of this period that has been eclipsed by the more familiar record of the Eastern seaboard. From 1769 to 1850 many entered the mission system, but few came out, most likely due to disease and culture shock. The resilience and re-forming of families and tribes is one of the positive stories that we hope will finally be told by researchers and documentarians in years to come.

Rediscovery

The missions, most fallen to ruin, were rediscovered and restored in the late 1800s and became historic tourist attractions, sparking enormous interest in California's Spanish and Mexican past. The primitive red clay tiles, and adobe bricks, the hewed wooden beams and cast bronze bells created a strong imagery for people looking for a new start in a land where it seemed like fantasies could come true. Books such as Helen Hunt Jackson's 1884 novel *Ramona*, romanticized this Spanish, Mexican, and Native American heritage, and became hugely popular. An early Native American activist, author Jackson, along with Abbott Kinney (who developed Venice, California) reported to Congress to try to obtain property rights and protection for the remaining Native Americans against the hordes of new settlers, but Jackson died in 1885, before achieving her goals. Ironically her book only brought more attention to California, and led to an increased migration west, sparking the next population explosion as well as tourists seeking the birthplace of "Ramona" and other fictionalized places. Interest in recreating this idealized version of the ol' Mission days in architecture started the Mission Revival movement (1885-1915), along with the somewhat related Craftsman or Mission style of architecture and furnishings (1905-1915). What emerged from these movements, perhaps as an antidote to the more stern Mission style, was a long lasting and resonant architectural movement, the Spanish Revival (1915-1940), sometimes referred to as the Spanish Colonial Revival, sparking a national trend in housing, furnishings, art, and lifestyle that began in California, and continues to this day.

Revival

San Diego, home to the first mission, is also considered the official birthplace of the Spanish Revival style in architecture, kicked off by the Panama-California International Exhibition, held in 1915. Visitors were inspired by the grandeur of Bertram Goodhue's Spanish Baroque tile-domed buildings that housed the exhibition events. The bright tile colors reflected the sunny skies, blue water, and all the vivid hues of nature. This innovative "new-old" style inspired architects to explore Mediterranean, European, Moorish, Spanish, and Mexican architecture and recombine them to create a world class style that would be adopted in a vast range of residential and commercial buildings across the country by the nation's leading architects.

Innovations and sub-genres made for even more interest as Spanish Colonial Revival, Monterey Revival, Mediterranean, Baroque, Gothic, and others influenced and informed the decorative and fine arts of the period.

Elements

The familiar structural elements used in Spanish Revival architecture included beamed ceilings, white stucco walls, arcades, patios, balconies, porches, hardwood floors, arches, outdoor rooms, water features, and courtyards. Wrought ironwork on gates, balconies, windows, railings, lighting, and in many other decorative forms; turned and spindled wooden touches, and carved stone and stucco, added weight and texture. Tile—both roofing and decorative—in the form of pavers to line pathways and verandas; and decorative vividly colored patterned versions to top fountains, cover benches, walls, fireplaces, and stair risers, are

another major component. Throughout it all, there was a love of color. Studies today indicate that bright and lively colors may have an important influence on people's moods, and that those with lots of color in their homes tend to have a more positive mood than people in neutral-toned environments. An adaptation from our berry-seeking hunter-gatherer ancestors? All we know is that it's a commonly heard refrain among California pottery collectors; they feel enlivened just by living with their collections.

Color-saturated pottery was a staple in the garden and throughout the house bringing the California nature colors indoors. The aptly named *Hispano Moresque* tile style was the most popular, with ceramic production in the state accomplished by over forty different companies. (One tile company even adopted the name Hispano Moresque.) Brightly colored Mexican textiles were used for curtains and tablecloths, pillows, and throws. California's year round temperate climate and indoor-outdoor lifestyle gave rise to its famous patio culture and reflected an air of informality that's still alive and well today. Even on the East Coast, where outdoor living cannot be achieved year 'round, the barbeque culture has inspired many an outdoor living room or outdoor kitchen, where people invest sums in the six figures on these outdoor rooms.

TERMINOLOGY:
MAKERS, ARTISTS, TRENDS AND STYLE

The major emphasis in this book is on the vintage decorative arts and interior furnishings made (primarily in California) from the 1920s through the 1940s. Unless otherwise stated, assume an item is made during the period of this study. If a description or caption includes the terms "reproduction," "new," or "recent," it most likely refers to something that is contemporary, i.e. made within the last twenty years. Though this text is not intended as a complete reference to makers and techniques, we list here some of the major companies, creators, and terms used in this book. (See *Bibliography* for further study.)

AET/American Encaustic Tile Co.: tile, 1919-1933, Vernon, Hermosa Beach. Parent company located in Zanesville, OH. Wide range of faience to fabricated tiles, famous for "kaospar" vitrified tiles.

Batchelder: tile, 1909-1932, Pasadena and Los Angeles. One of the largest tile makers, which sold throughout the country. Started production during the Arts and Crafts era utilizing dusty-looking, matt and earth tone glazing. Often still found in fireplace surrounds in vintage homes. Known for storefronts, pools, soda fountains, and water fountains similar to the one seen today at the Pasadena Playhouse.

Bauer Pottery: pottery, 1920s-1960s, Los Angeles. The J.A. Bauer Pottery Company made hand thrown art pottery vases, garden pots, and dinnerware. Bauer was a staple in many homes for decades prior to the advent of imported ceramics. A California classic that emerged from the state's patio-culture, it is known today primarily for brilliantly colored mix-and-match dinnerware, called ring ware. Urban myth hints that an innovative hostess used Bauer flowerpot saucers for a backyard dinner party and started a trend. The company caught on when they sold out of plant saucers and decided to make colorful plates and accessories to meet the demand. Artists in clay such as Matt Carlton and Fred Johnson designed and created hand thrown art vases, candleholders, handled floor pots, wavy edged flower pots, carnation jars, and more for the home and garden. Solid color dinnerware was copied by competitor Homer Laughlin in their Fiesta line. Many other industrial artware companies followed suit such as Gladding McBean, Metlox, Pacific, Vernon Kilns, and Meyer's California Rainbow.

Brayton Laguna: pottery and tile, 1927-1968, Laguna Beach. Founded by Durlin E. Brayton on Pacific Coast Highway. Pastel colored mix and match dinnerware with a hefty and handmade look, a wide variety of individually produced graphic pictorial tiles usually executed in a raised line style.

Also made figurines, most notably for Disney.

California Art Tile: tile, 1922-1956 Richmond, CA. Used many different decorating techniques, scenics predominate, usually found in with soft earthen tones.

California Faience: pottery and tile, 1915-1950, Berkeley, CA. Generally single glazed pottery, an early matte approach gave way to a high gloss and brightly colored glazes more suitable for the Spanish style home. Very high quality; bookends, trivets, and tile and copper combinations can be found.

Calco/California Clay Products: tile, 1923-1932, Vernon, South Gate, CA. A high quality maker of many styles and designs of tile, founded by master ceramist Rufus Keeler after his tenure at Gladding, McBean and prior to his arrival at Malibu Potteries. Many patterns repeat at Malibu with minor differences and it can be difficult to tell them apart.

Catalina or Catalina Island Pottery and Tile: 1927-1937, Avalon, CA. The Catalina Clay Products Company, under the watchful management of DM Renton, and with the financial wherewithal of William Wrigley, made utilitarian tile, art tile, and pottery of a very high quality for under 10 years, and in a short time built a town from the ground up using Catalina clay and minerals. Refers only to pottery and tile made at Pebbly Beach on Catalina Island and not "Catalina Pottery" made in Los Angeles by Gladding McBean. Also not to be confused with the generic phraseology "Catalina style" which indicates a certain period and look, one that certainly falls under the California Revival banner. One of the most diverse and original of the Golden Era makers, they produced a myriad of unique forms and designs, as well as beautiful and functional decorative housewares, numerous lines of complete dinnerware sets, and novelties. The imagery and rich glazes were inspired by the sea, ocean life, birds, plants, and the Spanish and Mexican Revival styles that were so popular then as now. Known as the quality pottery, it was sold in the best department stores throughout the country, as well as at various shops on the island, and was even sent to President Roosevelt's vacation home. Catalina tile was distributed through wholesalers in Los Angeles to builders and architects, and was installed at the Pomona colleges, in a Spanish style housing development in Long Beach, at the Arizona Biltmore, and in many private homes. Major furniture manufacturers put Catalina tiles on their popular tables, just as Monterey furniture topped their Prohibition Bar with Toyon Red and black Catalina tiles. (See Carole Coates' book *Catalina Island Pottery & Tile: Island Treasures* for more information.)

Catalina Pottery: pottery only, Glendale, California, 1937-1942. Produced on the mainland by Gladding, McBean & Co. (sometimes called GMB) after they bought the Catalina name and some molds. Used different glazes than the Island made wares, often two-toned with an ink stamp mark that reads "Made in U.S.A." , in pastel shades.

Cellini Craft: wrought aluminum and tile, 1934-1942, Illinois. Made trays and serving pieces sometimes inset with California tiles.

Ceramists: usually college educated men with degrees in mineralogy and chemistry who created clay and glaze formulations that were then applied to hand thrown pottery pieces, hand glazed or mass produced tiles, or sprayed on industrialized art ware. They were seen as skilled artists, sometimes designers, often manufacturers who owned their own companies, or they were commissioned, borrowed or "loaned," and were a sought after commodity in the boom times of the ceramic industry, which peaked in the 1930s.

Claycraft: tile, 1921-1939, Los Angeles. Founded by Fred H. Robertson. Geometrics, Moresque, ships, Spanish Colonial themes, wooded scenes, sconces, many techniques used from high gloss/high line technique to a matt rustic finish.

Cold painted: a technique using oil paints to decorate scenes or designs on previously glazed or bisque (unglazed) pottery and tiles.

Cuenca and Cuerda Seca: two of the most commonly used terminologies used to describe tile involving the decorative glazing methodology respectively "raised line" and "dry line."

D. & M.: tile, 1928-1939, Los Angeles. Spanish Moorish designs, painterly pictorial scenes with a brightly colored yet soft focus. Possibly manufactured tiles for Hispano Moresque, with similar looking designs. Frequent commercial use in Los Angeles and environs.

Decart/Decorative Arts Inc.: tile, 1927-1933, Hawthorne. Tile made with decal/transfer decorations on a thin white bisque tile body. Made advertising tiles as well.

Depression glazed: tile technique usually used with terra cotta paver tiles where a depression accepts colored glaze and is then fired.

Design influences in pottery, tile, and decor include Mexican, Spanish, Mayan-Aztec, Mediterranean, Moorish, Mission, Egyptian, Tunisian, Western, Pioneer, Native American, Art Deco, Japanese, Arts & Crafts.

Garden City Pottery: pottery, 1902-1979, San Jose, CA. Solid colored vases, oil jars, dinnerware and all manner of well-executed forms, started by making stoneware. Very popular garden ware line distributed mostly in the Northern California and Sacramento area. *Not* to be confused with San Jose Workshops' various studios in San Antonio, Texas.

Gladding, McBean & Company: pottery, tile, and architectural elements, 1873-1942, formerly in Glendale, and now based in Lincoln, CA. From huge garden urns and statuary, architectural building facades, to delicate Franciscan pottery and painterly tile mural installations, to sewer pipe and roofing tiles. The king of California potteries, they acquired Tropico (1923)and AET (1933) tile companies, and Catalina Island Pottery works (1937), and are still in existence today. They have begun to reissue classic designs in garden urns and other decorative pieces. Don't miss their yearly May tour and "open house."

Glaze painted: glaze is applied in a painterly technique on top of a glazed ceramic surface and then re-fired so it becomes a permanent part of the piece.

Golden Era: the Pre World War II California movement, which encompassed the Spanish Revival arts and crafts era. A magical place and time brought artists, architects, designers and ceramists together with the end result being the creation of many enduring art forms.

Hillside Pottery: pottery with tile, 1920s-1930s, North Hollywood, CA. Cement formed garden pots, urns, birdbaths, and fountains with incorporated mosaic tiles or shards in patterns. Other roadside makers in the state created wall plaques, flowerpots, cubes, and benches. Recent reproductions have been made, some with older tiles.

Hispano Moresque: tile, 1927-1934, Los Angeles. Refers to both a decorative style used in tile design, or the Tile Company, perhaps a distributor of tiles rather than a manufacturer but known for high quality decorative floral, and Moorish designs with matching border styles, suitable for home or business.

Imperial, Coronado, Del Rey or Monterey "style" furniture: many other manufacturers of the period made Spanish and Mexican style and Rancho furniture, some with painted finishes, many in similar forms. Imperial is usually unmarked (other than paper labels or branded model numbers), Coronado is sometimes marked. All have distinctive characteristics that the seasoned collector will recognize. (See *Monterey Furniture* chapter for more information.)

Iron and metal work: hand wrought or machine turned, this can vary from forged or cast , copper, bronze, brass, from ornate to simple.

Kraftile: tile, 1926-1997 Niles, CA. Made high-fired tiles in various patterns as well as murals, fountains, and huge panels. Can be found in and around San Francisco in many public and private installations.

Malibu Potteries: tile and pottery, 1926-1932, Malibu, CA.. Financed by May Rindge, headed by the top ceramist of the day, Rufus Keeler, Malibu was a short lived but important high quality producer of tiles (and a limited amount of pottery) for both home and commercial applications. Distinguished by elegant designs and rich glazes executed in many different styles. Today, May's daughter's home, the historic Adamson House-Malibu Lagoon Museum, is a tile shrine and a time capsule of the period, visited by enthusiasts of California's artistic legacy. Reproductions of Malibu's now-iconic designs are made today by modern artisans using old techniques.

Mexican Pottery and Tile: Talavera, Burnished, Tlaquepaque, Tonalå, and many fine artists beyond the scope of this study.

Mexican Tourist style: knick-knacks, souvenirs, wax figures, straw mosaics, crackleware, and lacquerware.

Monterey furniture: (See *Monterey* chapter.)

Monterey Paintings/"Juan Intenoche": a mystery artist/artists who created specialty designs and paintings for Mason's Monterey furniture line in the 1930s. There is no current documentation that a person with the actual name "Juan Intenoche" (which means nocturnal or could be construed as meaning a moonlighter) existed. It's possible that it is a pseudonym, or a comic name meaning "Juan Last Night," as in: "It wasn't me that was out dancing all night, it was Juan Intenoche!" It is believed that whoever "Juan" actually was, he conceived the idea of using comical Mexican images on furniture and plaques (some of them today are considered stereotypical) and became the head of Mason's painting department. It's possible that he signed off on other artists' work done in the style he created. Some Monterey paintings are not signed and these are of varying quality. This artist might have been an animator who worked for Disney during the Hyperion Studio days, as did many talented artists of the period. (Visit www.findingjuanintenoche.com for the latest research into the possible artists who could be the "Juan" we are looking to identify.)

Pacific Pottery Company: pottery, 1920-1942, Los Angeles. Produced a full *Hostessware* dinnerware line similar to Bauer but with more intense and varied glazing, as well as a full high quality artware line, some decorated in innovative underglaze lines and patterns, and a slipcast artware line.

Patio culture: the 1940s brought the birth of the BBQ, colorful pottery, and indoor-outdoor living inspired by the California climate, and which continues to this day throughout the country, as is evidenced by the latest trend towards "outdoor kitchens."

Plein Air: a style of painting that takes place outdoors, "in the air," with natural light.

Ranch Style home: a popular style in the 1920s through to the 1960s and to this day. Sometimes called the "California Ranch" it is considered to be an indigenous folk-architectural style, based on the simple lines of the Hispanic Colonial haciendas built during the Spanish rancho days, but with added Anglo farmhouse, or modern touches.

Reproduction iron/framework or bases: wrought iron in either mural or table form, lighting, and accessories made to imitate the style of an earlier period or of a particular artist or craftsman. Ironwork on wall murals is often reproduction since vintage iron frames would be considered too plain for today's homes.

Reproduction tile: many fine tile makers today recreate vintage styles and glazes, some as close replicas, others as interpretations of vintage designs, and entirely new designs with a vintage feel. The highest quality California Revival style tiles are still made in California by artisans utilizing the hand glazing methods of the earlier craftsmen. (Visit www.californiarevival.com for resources.)

Reproduction pottery: recently made pottery, dishware, or garden wares. Examples made today include copies of Bauer, Hillside, Fiesta, and others.

S & S/Solon and Schemmel: tile, 1920-1936; San Jose, CA. Used very strong colors and unusual motifs. Decorative and representational tiles, perhaps most famous are the fish tiles that were installed at the old Steinhart Aquarium (no longer extant) in Golden Gate Park.

San Jose Workshops: tile and pottery, 1927-1977, San Antonio, Texas and Mexico. A designation that refers to tiles and pottery including but not limited to *San Jose Mission, San Jose Pottery, Mexican Arts and Crafts, Mission Crafts, The Southern Company, and LAMOSA*. Ethel Wilson Harris, fondly known as Miz Harrie (1893-1984), was director of many of these firms over the years and exceptional designs in tile were produced during her tenures. Understandably confused as originating from San Jose, *California*, other independent Texas tile makers of this era can also exhibit similar looks and origins, such as work by Harding Black. Be aware of contemporary reproductions. These tiles are related to the California Revival movement owing to their Mexican themes, a painterly approach to scenes, and colorful primary color glazes (brought to Texas by a Californian named Frank Henderson). California and Texas also share a border with Mexico, and a common Franciscan Mission heritage dating back to the 1700s.

Spanish Revival: the return to California's design roots began with the Panama-California Exhibition, held in San Diego in 1915. Visitors loved the Spanish Baroque style of architecture, created by Bertram Goodhue, which included tile domed buildings. The bright tile colors seemed to reflect the sunny sky, blue water, as well as the soul of California. An explosion of innovation and combinations followed, other sub-genres proliferated, greatly influencing and informing the decorative and fine arts of the period from 1915 to 1940. (See *Spanish Revival: A Brief History*.)

Style: in the style of, normally meant as a version of, but not actually created by the original maker.

Taylor Tilery: tile, 1930-1941, Santa Monica, CA. Prolific company known for many different bird scenics, landscapes, and Hispanic themes. They employed many different artists over the years and incorporated a variety of different styles and looks, from matt to high gloss, from stylized to painterly with great success.

Tea tile: a tile with glazed sides or small feet, designed to be used as a trivet or a stand-alone decoration.

Tudor Potteries: tile and pottery, 1927-1939, Los Angeles. Made Hispano styled blurry tiles with great colors and interesting primitive, almost intentionally messy designs. After the so-called "death of tile" in the mid 1930s they transitioned into a line of pottery called *Hollywoodware*.

Vintage: old and authentic, not recently made, or "in the style of" or "vintage style." This distinction is important when determining value and when considering purchases.

BIBLIOGRAPHY

Baizerman, Suzanne, Lynn Downey, and John Toki. *Fired By Ideals. Arequipa Pottery and the Arts and Crafts Movement*. November 2000 exhibition held at the Oakland Museum of California. Rohnert Park, CA: Pomegranate Communications, Inc., 2000.

California Heritage Museum. *California Tile, The Golden Era 1910-1940*, Vol. 1-2. Joseph Taylor, Steven Soukup, Michael Trotter, editors. Atglen, PA: Schiffer Publishing Ltd., 2004.

_____. *Monterey Furnishings of California's Spanish Revival*. Roger Renick and Michael Trotter, editors. Atglen, PA: Schiffer Publishing Ltd., 2000.

Chase, J. Smeaton, and Charles F. Saunders. *The California Padres and Their Missions*, Boston and New York: Houghton Mifflin Co., 1915.

Chipman, Jack. *Collector's Encyclopedia of California Pottery*, Second Edition, Paducah, KY: Collector Books, 1999.

Cook III, S.F. "Jerry", and Tina Skinner. *Spanish Revival Architecture*, Atglen, PA: Schiffer Publishing Ltd., 2005.

Coates, Carole. *Catalina Island Pottery and Tile: 1927 – 1937: Island Treasures*. Atglen, PA: Schiffer Publishing Ltd., 2001.

Elliott-Bishop, James F., *Franciscan, Catalina, and other Gladding, McBean Wares, Ceramic Table and Art Wares: 1873-1942*. Atglen, PA: Schiffer Publishing Ltd., 2001.

Fridley, Al. *Catalina Pottery: The Early Years, 1927-1937*. Los Angeles: A.W. Fridley. 1977.

Gebhard, Patricia. *George Washington Smith: Architect of the Spanish Colonial Revival*. Layton, UT: Gibbs Smith, 2005.

Gellner, Arrol. *Red Tile Style, America's Spanish Revival Architecture*. New York: Viking Studio, a member of Penguin Putnam Inc., 2002.

George Washington Smith: An Architects Scrapbook. Marc Appleton, editor. Tailwater Press, 2001.

Gleason, Duncan. *The Islands and Ports of California*. New York: The Devin-Adair Co., 1958.

Habig, Marion A., *The Alamo Chain of Mission: A History of San Antonio's Five Old Missions*. Chicago: Franciscan Herald Press, 1976.

Harris, Larry. *The Jewels of Avalon, Decorative Tiles of Catalina Island*. 1999.

Historic Mission Inn. Barbara Moore, editor. Riverside, CA: Friends of the Mission Inn, 1998.

Hillinger, Charles. *Charles Hillinger's Channel Islands*. Santa Barbara: Santa Cruz Island Foundation. 1999.

Hoefs, Steven and Aisha. *Catalina Island Pottery Collectors Guide*. 1993.

Jackson, Helen Hunt. *Glimpses of California and the Missions*. Boston: Little, Brown and Co., 1911.

_____. *Ramona*. New York: Grosset and Dunlap, 1912.

_____. *A Century of Dishonor*. New York: Harper & Brothers, 1885.

Kanner, Diane. *Wallace Neff and the Grand Houses of the Golden State*. New York: The Monacelli Press, 2005.

Karlson, Norman. *American Art Tile, 1876-1941*. New York: Rizzoli International Publications Inc., 1998.

_____. *The Encyclopedia of American Art Tiles*. Volumes 3 and 4. Atglen, PA: Schiffer Publishing Ltd, 2005.

Masson, Kathryn. *Santa Barbara Style*. New York: Rizzoli International Publications, Inc., 2001.

May, Cliff. *Sunset Western Ranch Houses*. In collaboration with the staff of Sunset Magazine. San Francisco, CA: Lane Publishing Company, 1946.

_____. *Western Ranch Houses by Cliff May*. Menlo Park, California: Lane Publishing Co.,1958.

McMillian, Elizabeth. *Casa California: Spanish Style Houses from Santa Barbara to San Clemente*. New York: Rizzoli International Publications Inc., 1996.

_____. *California Colonial, The Spanish and Ranch Revival Styles*. Atglen, PA: Schiffer Publishing Ltd., 2002.

McWilliams, Carey. *California, The Great Exception*. Berkeley and Los Angeles: University of California Press, 1949.

Pasquali, Jim. *Sandfords Guide to Garden City Pottery: A Hidden Treasure of Northern California*. Adelmore Press, 1999.

Renton, D.M. Autobiography. 1939. From *Santa Catalina Island: It's Magic, People and History* by Ernest Windle. (1931)

Rindge, Ronald L., *Ceramic Art of the Malibu Potteries 1926-1932*. Malibu, CA: The Malibu Lagoon Museum, 1988,

_____. More about Malibu Potteries 1926-1932. Malibu, CA: The Malibu Lagoon Museum, 1997.

Rosenthal, Lee. *Catalina Tiles of the Magic Isle*. Sausalito, CA: Windgate Press, 1992.

Sexton, R.W., *Spanish Influence on American Architecture and Decoration*. New York: Brentano's, 1927.

Shorts, Don Allen. *George Mason and the Story of Monterey Furniture*. Ventura, CA: The Old California Store, 1998.

Snyder, Jeffrey B., *Beautiful Bauer: A Pictorial Study with Prices*. Atglen, PA: Schiffer Publishing Ltd., 2000.

Starr, Kevin. *California*. New York: Modern Library, 2005.

_____. *Inventing the Dream, California Through the Progressive Era*. New York: Oxford University Press, Inc., 1985.

Stern, Bill. *California Pottery: From Missions to Modernism*. San Francisco: Chronicle Books, 2001.

Street-Porter, Tim. *Casa Mexicana*. New York: Stewart, Tabori, and Chang, 1994.

Torres, Louis. *San Antonio Missions*. Tucson, Arizona: Southwest Parks and Monuments Association, 1993.

Tuchman, Mitch. *Bauer, Classic American Pottery*. San Francisco, California: Chronicle Books, 1995.

Wallace Neff, The Romance of Regional Architecture. Andrea P.A. Belloti, editor. San Marino, California: The Huntington Library,1989.

White, William S., and Steven K. Tice. *Santa Catalina Island: It's Magic, People and History*. 2nd Edition. Glendora, California: White Limited Editions, 2000.

Windle, Ernest. *Windle's History of Catalina Island*. Avalon, California: The Catalina Islander publ., 1931.

Zimmerman, William, Jr., *William Wrigley, Jr.: The Man and His Business 1861-1932*. Chicago: Private Printing. 1935.

Articles, Brochures, and Catalogues

Barker Brothers. *Monterey Furniture created by Barker Brothers for California Homes*. Brochure. Los Angeles: Sterling Press, 1933.

Bush, Jennifer. "Colorful Catalina: Antique tiles and pottery from the Island fetch a high price." *Orange County Register Home*, vol 5, Issue 8, August 2004. Santa Ana, CA: OCR Magazines, 2004.

_____. "Pottery Pioneer: Laguna's Brayton ceramic shop is gone, but its work is far from forgotten," *Orange Country Register*, Home and Garden, January 29, 2005. Santa Ana, CA: OCR 2005

Collins, Nancy. "Diane Keaton, The Actress's 1920s Bel Air House is a California Classic,"

Architectural Digest vol 62, Number 4, April 2005. Los Angeles: The Condé Nast Publications Inc., 2005.

_____. "Diane Keaton, The Actress and Director Restores her Wallace Neff residence in Beverly Hills," *Architectural Digest* vol 56, Number 7, July 1999. Los Angeles, The Condé Nast Publications Inc., 1999

De Turenne, Veronique. "The Tile Detectives: They're on the case to save vintage California tile from a remodel-mad world." *Los Angeles Times*, Home sec F, October 14, 2004. Los Angeles, 2004.

Flood, Elizabeth Clair. "Monterey Furniture", *Cowboys and Indians* Vol 5, Number 1, Salt Lake City, UT: Reid Slaughter, Publisher. March 1997.

Frost, Susan Toomey. "San Jose and Miz Harrie, Texas Tile with a Mission". *Tile Heritage*, Vol. II, No. 2. Pgs 19-25. Healdsburg, CA.

Finch, Christopher. "Antiques: Monterey Furniture, Pieces that Recall Ranch Life and Hispanic Tradition," *Architectural Digest* vol 53, Number 6, June 1996. Los Angeles: The Condé Nast Publications Inc., 1996.

Gladding, McBean and Co. Pottery and Price List, 1932. San Francisco: Taylor and Taylor.

Pacific Pottery Catalog and Price List, Pacific Clay Products Company, Los Angeles: 1934.

Santa Monica Heritage Museum (now California Heritage Museum). *Monterey: An Exhibition of California Rancho Furniture, Pottery, and Art*, June 2-July 31, 1988. Santa Monica, CA: 1990.

Simpson, Jeffrey. "California Art Tiles, The Enduring Appeal of the Golden State's Legacy of Color and Design," *Architectural Digest* vol 62, Number 6, June 2005. Los Angeles: The Condé Nast Publications Inc., 2005.

Slack, Steve. "Old Monterey". *Country Home*, July/August 1998.

Interviews and Oral Histories:

All interviews conducted by Carole Coates either in person, via telephone, or email unless otherwise stated.
Connors, Betsy. 2006.
Dempster, John. 2002 and 2006.
Graves, Maxine. 2000-2006
Kaiser, Brian. 2000.
Langdon, Sue Ann.1999 and 2006
Lopez, Pastor Sr., Avalon. 2000.
Renton, Dave. 2000-2006.
Shorts, Don. 1998-2006.
Upton, Roger Jr., 2000.
Windle, Johnnie and Jean. Avalon.1998.

Resources:

Visit www.californiarevival.com or www.findingjuanintenoche.com for the latest information, to contribute information, or make inquiries.